P9-EES-376

Baking
Is
Fun

Volume 9

Recipes No. 679 - 750

ISBN 0-9691357-9-3

Printed and Bound in Canada

*I*ntroduction

Dear Reader:

Thank you for purchasing the 9th Volume in our series, "Baking is Fun".

Tempt your palate and enjoy the magnificent colour photographs as you leaf through this 128 page book. We have gathered, tested and selected only the most delicious assortment of recipes for you.

Treat yourself, your family and friends to a wonderful variety of enticing desserts. This volume includes: Fancy Tortes; Cakes, Slices and Rolls; Pastries; Cold and Warm Desserts. It will be difficult to decide which of the 72 recipes you should prepare first. Irregardless of where you begin, we are confident that you will be delighted with the results.

Go ahead, select a recipe and begin your culinary journey!

We wish you joyful baking.

Additional copies of this book may be obtained by writing to:

oetker Recipe Service
2229 Drew Road
Mississauga, Ontario
L5S 1E5

Contents

Fancy Tortes

Pear Torte

Birnentorte

Recipe No. 679

Dough:

190 g	all-purpose flour	1½ cups
65 g	icing sugar, sifted	½ cup
1	egg yolk	1
15 mL	milk	1 tbsp
85 g	butter, cold	⅓ cup

Cream Cheese Filling:

3	ripe pears, finely chopped	3
45 mL	pear liqueur	3 tbsp
250 g	cream cheese	1 cup
125 g	icing sugar, sifted	1 cup
1 pkg	**oetker** vanilla sugar (9 g)	1 pkg
	juice of 1 lemon	
½ btl	**oetker** lemon flavouring concentrate (1 mL)	½ btl
6 sheets	**oetker** gelatin sheets	6 sheets
250 mL	whipping cream	1 cup

Topping:

250 mL	whipping cream	1 cup
30 mL	icing sugar, sifted	2 tbsp
1 pkg	**oetker** Whip it (10 g)	1 pkg

Decoration:

16	pear slices, canned	16
32	chocolate curls	32
100 g	almonds, sliced	¾ cup

Dough:

GREASE a 24-25 cm (9-10") springform pan.
SIFT flour onto a working surface.
MAKE a well in the centre. Put icing sugar, egg yolk, and milk in the well.
CUT butter in small pieces over the ingredients in the well.
COVER with flour.
STARTING from the centre, work ingredients into a smooth dough. Chill for 1 hour.
PREHEAT oven to 200°C (400°F).
PRESS two-thirds of the dough into the bottom of the prepared pan.
PRESS remaining dough around inside rim of pan to form sides 3 cm (1¼") high.
PRICK dough with a fork.
BAKE for 20 minutes.
CAREFULLY remove from pan. Cool completely.

Cream Cheese Filling:

PLACE pears in a bowl and cover with pear liqueur. Chill.
IN a mixing bowl, combine cream cheese, icing sugar, vanilla sugar, lemon juice and flavouring concentrate. Beat until smooth.
DISSOLVE gelatin according to package directions.
IN another bowl, beat whipping cream to stiff peaks.
FOLD gelatin and whipped cream into the cream cheese mixture gently but thoroughly.
WHEN cream cheese mixture begins to set, fold in marinated pears.
TURN mixture into cooled crust. Smooth surface. CHILL for 1 hour.

Topping:

IN a mixing bowl, beat whipping cream, icing sugar and Whip it to stiff peaks.
SPREAD whipped cream mixture evenly over the top and sides of cake.
DECORATE with pear slices and chocolate curls.
GENTLY press sliced almonds into the side of the cake.

9

Strawberry Charlotte

Erdbeercharlotte

Recipe No. 680

Ingredients:

250 g	strawberries, halved	2 cups
500 g	cream cheese	2 cups
200 g	icing sugar, sifted	1³/₄ cups
2 pkgs	**oetker** vanilla sugar (18 g)	2 pkgs
¹/₂ btl	**oetker** lemon flavouring concentrate (1 mL)	¹/₂ btl
5 drops	**oetker** rum flavouring concentrate	5 drops
	juice of 1 lemon	
500 mL	strawberries, pureed	2 cups
12 sheets	**oetker** gelatin sheets	12 sheets
50-60	savoiardi biscuits	50-60

Glaze:

1 pkg	**oetker** instant clear glaze (30 g)	1 pkg

Decoration:

250 mL	whipping cream	1 cup

LIGHTLY grease and line a bowl (26 cm/10" in diameter and 9 cm/3.5" deep) with waxed paper (two layers thick) 50 cm (20") long.
LINE the bottom of the bowl with strawberries.
IN a mixing bowl, combine cream cheese, icing sugar, vanilla sugar, flavouring concentrates, lemon juice and pureed strawberries. Beat until smooth.
PREPARE gelatin according to package directions.
FOLD into the cream cheese mixture gently but thoroughly. Allow to set slightly.
TURN one-half of the mixture into the bowl.
POSITION savoiardi biscuits around the edge of the bowl.
FILL bowl with remaining mixture. (You may have to trim the biscuits.)
TOP with remaining biscuits.
REFRIGERATE for 3 hours.
DIP bowl in hot water. Loosen the edges with a knife and by pulling gently on the waxed paper. Invert onto a serving plate.

Glaze:
PREPARE glaze according to package directions.
GLAZE dessert.

Decoration:
BEAT whipping cream to stiff peaks.
DECORATE top and sides of charlotte.

Almond-Quark Torte

Mandel-Topfentorte

Recipe No. 681

Batter:

8	egg yolks	8
150 g	icing sugar, sifted	1¹/₃ cups
1 pkg	**oetker** vanilla sugar (9 g)	1 pkg
250 g	almonds, ground	2¹/₂ cups
	juice and peel of ¹/₂ lemon	
100 g	quark	¹/₂ cup
75 mL	zucchini, grated	¹/₃ cup
	and strained	
5 mL	cinnamon	1 tsp
4	egg whites	4
15 mL	bread crumbs	1 tbsp

Topping:

4	egg whites	4
50 g	sugar	¹/₄ cup

Batter:
PREHEAT oven to 200°C (400°F). Grease a
20-23 cm (8-9") springform pan.
IN a mixing bowl, combine egg yolks, icing
sugar and vanilla sugar. Beat until fluffy.
ADD almonds, lemon juice, peel, quark,
zucchini and cinnamon. Fold in gently but
thoroughly.
BEAT egg whites to stiff peaks.
FOLD beaten egg whites and bread crumbs
into the quark mixture gently but thoroughly.
TURN mixture into prepared pan.
BAKE for 30 minutes.
REMOVE from pan. Cool completely.

Topping:
REDUCE oven temperature to 160°C (325°F).
BEAT egg whites and sugar to stiff peaks.
PLACE mixture in a pastry bag fitted with a
star tube.
DECORATE cake.
RETURN to oven.
BAKE for 10 minutes.

*F*laky Torte

Flockentorte

Recipe No. 682

Short Pastry:

160 g	all-purpose flour	1¼ cups
50 g	sugar	¼ cup
3 drops	**oetker** lemon flavouring concentrate	3 drops
½ pkg	**oetker** vanilla sugar (4.5 g)	½ pkg
110 g	butter, cold	½ cup

Choux Pastry:

250 mL	milk	1 cup
110 g	butter	½ cup
pinch	salt	pinch
135 g	all-purpose flour	1 cup
4	eggs	4

Streusel:

1 pkg	**oetker** German Streusel cake mix (425 g)	1 pkg
110 g	butter, softened	½ cup
1	egg	1

Cream Filling:

500 mL	whipping cream	2 cups
50 g	sugar	¼ cup
½ pkg	**oetker** vanilla sugar (4.5 g)	½ pkg
6 sheets	**oetker** gelatin sheets	6 sheets
50 mL	kirsch (cherry brandy)	¼ cup

Spreading:

| 175 mL | red currant jam | ¾ cup |

Decoration:

| 50 g | almonds, sliced | ½ cup |
| some | icing sugar, sifted | some |

Short Pastry:

SIFT flour onto a working surface.
MAKE a well in the centre. Put sugar, flavouring concentrate and vanilla sugar in the well.
CUT butter in small pieces over the ingredients in the well.
COVER with flour.
STARTING from the centre, work ingredients into a smooth dough.
CHILL for one-half hour.
PREHEAT oven to 190°C (375°F). Lightly grease and line with waxed paper the bottom of a 25 cm (10") springform pan.
PRESS dough evenly into the bottom of the springform pan.
BAKE for 8 minutes. Chill.

Choux Pastry:

IN a saucepan, bring milk, butter and salt to a boil.
REMOVE from heat and add flour all at once.
STIR over medium heat until mixture forms a ball around the spoon and pulls away from the side of the pan. (Do not overcook.)
COOL slightly.
ADD unbeaten eggs to dough, one at a time, stirring after each addition until smooth.
BEAT until mixture is shiny and no longer sticky.
CHILL until mixture holds its shape.
DIVIDE the choux into three.
SPREAD one-third of the mixture onto the bottom of a 25 cm (10") springform pan.

Streusel:

PREHEAT oven to 220°C (425°F).
PREPARE German Streusel according to package directions.
DIVIDE into three.
SPRINKLE one-third of the Streusel over the choux pastry.
BAKE for 12 minutes or until golden brown.
REMOVE from pan.
REPEAT choux/streusel steps twice.

Cream Filling:

IN a mixing bowl, beat whipping cream, sugar and vanilla sugar to stiff peaks.
PREPARE gelatin according to package directions.

FOLD gelatin and kirsch into the whipped cream mixture gently but thoroughly.
CHILL until mixture is thick enough to spread.

Spreading:
SPREAD red currant jam evenly over the baked short pastry.
TOP with one layer of choux/streusel.
SPREAD one-half of the whipped cream mixture evenly over the choux/streusel.
TOP with second layer of choux/streusel.
SPREAD remaining whipped cream mixture evenly over second layer.
TOP with remaining choux/streusel pastry layer.

Decoration:
GENTLY press sliced almonds into the side of the torte.
SPRINKLE with icing sugar.

Prague Cherry Torte

Prager Kirschtorte

Recipe No. 683

Batter:

4	egg yolks	4
220 g	butter or margarine, softened	1 cup
70 g	icing sugar, sifted	¹/₂ cup
1 pkg	**oetker** vanilla sugar (9 g)	1 pkg
100 g	milk chocolate, melted	3¹/₂ squares
4	egg whites	4
100 g	sugar	¹/₂ cup
5 mL	**oetker** baking powder	1 tsp
135 g	all-purpose flour	1 cup
125 g	hazelnuts, toasted, ground	1¹/₂ cups
5 mL	cinnamon	1 tsp
60 mL	rum	4 tbsp
1 jar	pitted sour cherries, well drained (796 mL/28 fl oz)	1 jar

Decoration:

	some icing sugar, sifted	some

Batter:

PREHEAT oven to 180°C (350°F). Line a 25 cm (10") springform pan with waxed paper.
IN a mixing bowl, combine egg yolks, butter or margarine, icing sugar and vanilla sugar. Beat until fluffy.
FOLD in chocolate gently but thoroughly.
BEAT egg whites and sugar to stiff peaks.
FOLD beaten egg whites into the egg yolk mixture gently but thoroughly.
IN another bowl, sift together baking powder and flour.
ADD hazelnuts, cinnamon and rum.
FOLD into the egg yolk mixture.
STIR in cherries.

TURN batter into prepared pan.
BAKE for 50-60 minutes.
TURN cake onto wire cooling rack. Cool completely.
LAY a stencil or doily over the cake. Sprinkle with icing sugar.

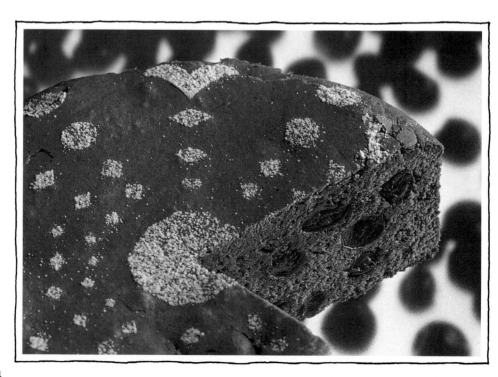

Iced Melon Torte

Geeiste Melonentorte

Recipe No. 684

Batter:
(See Recipe No. 691)

Filling:

¹/₂	honeydew melon	¹/₂	
5	egg yolks	5	
75 mL	honey	¹/₃	cup
60 mL	rum	4	tbsp
2 pkgs	**oetker** vanilla sugar (18 g)	2	pkgs
1 mL	cinnamon	¹/₄	tsp
8 sheets	**oetker** gelatin sheets	8	sheets
375 mL	whipping cream	1¹/₂	cups
¹/₂	honeydew melon, peeled, diced	¹/₂	
15 mL	Grand Marnier	1	tbsp
15 mL	honey	1	tbsp

Decoration:

100 g	semi-sweet chocolate	4	squares
125 mL	whipped cream,	¹/₂	cup

Batter:
PREPARE marzipan layer cake as directed on page 27.
LINE bottom and sides of a 25 cm (10") springform pan with slices of baked marzipan layer cake, 3 mm (¹/₈") thick.

Filling:
PEEL, seed and puree melon.
IN a mixing bowl, combine egg yolks, honey, rum, vanilla sugar and cinnamon.
BEAT until fluffy.
FOLD in pureed melon gently but thoroughly.
PREPARE gelatin according to package directions. Fold into melon mixture. Chill.
IN another bowl, beat whipping cream to stiff peaks.
WHEN melon mixture begins to set, fold in whipped cream and cubed melon pieces.
ADD Grand Marnier and honey.
TURN melon mixture into prepared pan.
CHILL in freezer for 24 hours.

Decoration:
MELT chocolate in a double boiler.
PLACE in a pastry bag fitted with a small, fine tube.
PIPE designs onto a piece of parchment paper and refrigerate until firm.
DECORATE torte with chocolate and whipped cream.

Glazed Orange Torte

Ladinische Orangentorte

Recipe No. 685

Batter:

6	egg yolks	6
150 g	icing sugar, sifted	1¹/₂ cups
	juice of 1 lemon	
1 pkg	**oetker** vanilla sugar (9 g)	1 pkg
¹/₂ btl	**oetker** lemon flavour-	¹/₂ btl
	ing concentrate (1 mL)	
pinch	salt	pinch
6	egg whites	6
50 g	sugar	¹/₄ cup
180 g	cream of wheat	1 cup

Filling:

some	orange jam	some
some	orange liqueur	some

Cream Topping:

250 mL	whipping cream	1 cup
45 mL	orange liqueur	3 tbsp
3 sheets	**oetker** gelatin sheets	3 sheets

Topping:

3-4	blood oranges	3-4

Glaze:

1 pkg	**oetker** instant clear glaze (30 g)	1 pkg

Batter:
PREHEAT oven to 180°C (350°F). Line a
25 cm (10") springform pan with waxed paper.
IN a mixing bowl, beat egg yolks, icing sugar,
lemon juice, vanilla sugar, flavouring
concentrate and salt until thick and fluffy.
IN another bowl, beat egg whites and sugar to
stiff peaks.
FOLD beaten egg whites and cream of wheat
into the egg yolk mixture gently but
thoroughly.
TURN into prepared pan.
BAKE for 40-45 minutes.
REMOVE from pan. Cool completely.
SLICE cake twice to make three layers.

Filling:
MIX together orange jam and orange liqueur.
SPREAD over surface of each layer.

Cream Topping:
BEAT whipping cream to stiff peaks.
STIR in orange liqueur.
PREPARE gelatin according to package
directions.
FOLD into whipped cream mixture and
refrigerate.
WHEN the cream begins to set, spread over
cake in a dome-like fashion
PEEL oranges and remove white skin. Slice.
DECORATE cake.

Glaze:
PREPARE glaze according to package
directions.
GLAZE cake. Chill until set.

Ricotta Torte

Ricottatorte

Recipe No. 686

Dough:

220 g	all-purpose flour	1²/₃ cups
50 g	icing sugar, sifted	¹/₂ cup
4	egg yolks	4
5 drops	**oetker** lemon flavour-ing concentrate	5 drops
45 mL	dry Marsala wine	3 tbsp
2 mL	salt	¹/₂ tsp
120 g	butter, softened	¹/₂ cup

Filling:

1 kg	ricotta cheese	4 cups
120 g	icing sugar, sifted	1 cup
2 mL	salt	¹/₂ tsp
1 pkg	**oetker** vanilla sugar (9 g) peel of ¹/₂ orange	1 pkg
4	egg yolks	4
30 g	raisins	¹/₄ cup
30 g	candied orange peel, diced	¹/₄ cup
30 g	candied lemon peel, diced	¹/₄ cup
50 g	almonds, sliced	¹/₃ cup

Brushing:

1	egg white, beaten	1

Dough:

GREASE a 25 cm (10") springform pan.
SIFT flour onto a working surface.
MAKE a well in the centre. Put icing sugar, egg yolks, flavouring concentrate, wine, salt and butter in the well.
STARTING from the centre, work ingredients into a smooth dough.
CHILL for 30 minutes.
PREHEAT oven to 180°C (350°F).
DIVIDE the dough in half.
PRESS one-half of the dough into the bottom of the prepared springform pan.
PRESS half of the remaining dough around the inside rim of the pan to form sides 3 cm (1¹/₄") high.
PRICK dough with fork several times.

Filling:

STRAIN ricotta cheese into a mixing bowl.
ADD icing sugar, salt, vanilla sugar, orange peel, egg yolks, raisins and candied orange and lemon peel to the strained ricotta. Mix well.
TURN ricotta mixture into the pan. Smooth surface.
SPRINKLE with sliced almonds.
ROLL remaining dough thinly. Cut into 2 cm (1") wide strips. Place in lattice pattern over the surface of the cake.
BRUSH evenly with egg white.
BAKE for 70 minutes.
COOL completely in pan.

Cherry Torte

Weichseltorte "Lady"

Recipe No. 687

Batter:

4	egg yolks	4
75 mL	honey	⅓ cup
30 mL	milk	2 tbsp
1 pkg	**oetker** vanilla sugar (9 g)	1 pkg
15 mL	rum	1 tbsp
120 g	wholewheat flour	1 cup
4	egg whites	4

Filling:

2	egg yolks	2
1 pkg	**oetker** vanilla sugar (9 g)	1 pkg
45 mL	honey	3 tbsp
	juice and peel of 1 lemon	
500 g	quark	2 cups
3 sheets	**oetker** gelatin sheets	3 sheets
15 mL	water	1 tbsp

Topping:

1	orange	1
1 can	cherry pie filling (398 mL/14 fl oz)	1 can

Decoration:

50 g	almonds, sliced	½ cup

Batter:
PREHEAT oven to 160°C (325°F).
GREASE a 23 cm (9") springform pan. Dust lightly with flour.
IN a mixing bowl, beat egg yolks, honey, milk, vanilla sugar and rum until thick and fluffy.
FOLD in flour gently but thoroughly.
BEAT egg whites to stiff peaks. Fold into the egg yolk mixture gently but thoroughly.
POUR batter into prepared pan. Smooth surface.
BAKE for 35-40 minutes.
REMOVE from pan. Cool completely.

Filling:
IN a mixing bowl, beat egg yolks, vanilla sugar, honey, lemon juice and peel until fluffy.
FOLD in quark gently but thoroughly.
PREPARE gelatin according to package directions.
ADD to quark mixture. Mix well. Refrigerate.
SLICE cake twice to make three layers.
SPREAD two-thirds of the quark mixture over top of the three layers. Assemble cake.
SPREAD remaining one-third of quark mixture over surface and sides of cake.

Topping:
PEEL and slice the orange.
ARRANGE around the rim of the cake.
SPREAD cherry pie filling evenly over the centre of the cake.
GENTLY press sliced almonds into the side of the cake.

Sweet and Sour Apple Torte

Renettentorte

Recipe No. 688

Dough:

250	g	wholewheat flour	2	cups
	pinch	salt		pinch
60	g	butter	$^1/_4$	cup
1		egg yolk	1	
80	g	sugar	$^1/_3$	cup
1	pkg	**oetker** vanilla sugar (9 g)	1	pkg
		peel of 1 lemon		
30-45	mL	milk	2-3	tbsp

Filling:

3		egg whites	3	
100	g	sugar	$^1/_2$	cup
120	g	nuts, ground	$1^1/_4$	cups
50	g	bread crumbs (first amount)	$^1/_3$	cup
1	mL	cinnamon	$^1/_4$	tsp
		peel of $^1/_2$ lemon		
5-6		apples, peeled, coarsely grated	5-6	
60	mL	cranberry jam	4	tbsp
30	mL	bread crumbs (second amount)	2	tbsp
		juice of $^1/_2$ lemon		

Dough:

GREASE a 25 cm (10") springform pan.
SIFT flour onto a working surface.
MAKE a well in the centre. Put salt, butter, egg yolk, sugar, vanilla sugar, lemon peel and milk in the well.
COVER with flour.
STARTING from the centre, work ingredients into a smooth dough.
CHILL for 1 hour.
PREHEAT oven to 200°C (400°F).
PRESS two-thirds of the dough into the bottom of the prepared pan.
PRESS remaining dough around the inside rim of the pan to form sides 3 cm ($1^1/_4$") high.
BAKE for 12 minutes.

Filling:

PREHEAT oven to 180°C (350°F).
BEAT egg whites and sugar to stiff peaks.
FOLD nuts, bread crumbs (first amount), cinnamon, lemon peel and two-thirds of the grated apples into the beaten egg whites gently but thoroughly.
SPREAD cranberry jam evenly over the surface of the baked dough.
SPRINKLE with bread crumbs (second amount).
DISTRIBUTE remaining grated apples over top of bread crumbs. Sprinkle with lemon juice.
TURN apple mixture over top of the grated apples in the pan.
BAKE for 40-50 minutes.

Mango-Kiwi Torte

Mango-Kiwi-Torte "Bernadotte"

Recipe No. 689

Batter:

6	egg yolks	6
200 g	sugar	1 cup
1 pkg	**oetker** vanilla sugar (9 g)	1 pkg
30 mL	milk	2 tbsp
1 btl	**oetker** rum flavouring concentrate (2 mL)	1 btl
6	egg whites	6
70 g	all-purpose flour	¹/₂ cup
15 mL	cocoa	1 tbsp
45 mL	**oetker** Gustin corn starch	3 tbsp
5 mL	**oetker** baking powder	1 tsp

Filling:

1 L	yogurt	4 cups
75 mL	honey	¹/₃ cup
some	lemon peel	some
12 sheets	**oetker** gelatin sheets	12 sheets
250 mL	whipping cream	1 cup
1 pkg	**oetker** vanilla sugar (9 g)	1 pkg

Topping:

1	ripe mango	1
3-4	kiwi	3-4

Glaze:

1 pkg	**oetker** instant clear glaze (30 g)	1 pkg

Batter:
PREHEAT oven to 180°C (350°F). Grease and flour a 25 cm (10") springform pan.
IN a mixing bowl, beat egg yolks, two-thirds of the sugar, vanilla sugar, milk and flavouring concentrate until thick and creamy.
IN another bowl, beat egg whites and remaining sugar to stiff peaks.
SIFT together flour, cocoa, cornstarch and baking powder.
FOLD beaten egg whites and flour mixture into the egg yolk mixture gently but thoroughly.
TURN batter into prepared pan.
BAKE for 45-50 minutes.
REMOVE from pan immediately. Cool completely.
SLICE cake in half to make two layers.

Filling:
IN a mixing bowl, combine yogurt, honey and lemon peel.
PREPARE gelatin according to package directions. Let cool slightly.
IN another bowl, beat whipping cream and vanilla sugar to stiff peaks.
FOLD gelatin and whipped cream into the yogurt mixture.
SPREAD one-half of the filling over the bottom layer. Top with second layer.
SPREAD remaining filling over surface and side of cake.

Topping:
PEEL and slice mango.
PEEL and slice kiwi.
DECORATE cake. (See photo.)

Glaze:
PREPARE glaze according to package directions.
GLAZE cake.

Ziller Valley Cranberry Cake

Zillertaler Beerenkuchen

Recipe No. 690

Batter:

625 mL	water	2½ cups	
	pinch salt		pinch
165 g	cream of wheat	1 cup	
1 pkg	**oetker** vanilla sugar (9 g)	1 pkg	
½ btl	**oetker** lemon flavour-ing concentrate (1 mL)	½ btl	
3	egg yolks	3	
3	egg whites	3	
120 g	sugar	⅔ cup	

Topping:

1 can	cranberry sauce (398 mL/14 fl oz)	1 can	

Glaze:

1 pkg	**oetker** instant clear glaze (30 g)	1 pkg	

Decoration:

250 mL	whipping cream	1 cup	
50 mL	cranberry sauce	¼ cup	

Batter:
GREASE and line a 23 cm (9") springform pan with waxed paper.

IN a saucepan, bring water and salt to a boil.
ADD cream of wheat while stirring constantly.
COOK over low heat for 20 minutes, stirring occasionally.
COVER and let rest for 30 minutes.
STIR in vanilla sugar, flavouring concentrate and egg yolks.
IN a mixing bowl, beat egg whites and sugar to stiff peaks.
FOLD beaten egg whites into cream of wheat mixture gently but thoroughly.
TURN mixture into prepared pan. Smooth surface with a knife.
PREHEAT oven to 175°C (350°F).

Topping:
SPOON cranberry sauce over cream of wheat mixture.
BAKE for 35-40 minutes.
PLACE cake on a wire cooling rack. Cool completely.

Glaze:
PREPARE glaze according to package directions.
SPOON carefully over cranberry sauce.

Decoration:
BEAT whipping cream to stiff peaks.
FOLD in cranberry sauce.
PLACE whipped cream mixture in a pastry bag fitted with a medium plain tube.

Marzipan Layer Cake

Baumkuchen

Recipe No. 691

Batter:

170 g	butter, softened	³/₄	cup
60 g	icing sugar, sifted	¹/₂	cup
100 g	marzipan	3.5	oz
8	egg yolks	8	
1 pkg	**oetker** vanilla sugar (9 g)	1	pkg
1 mL	allspice	¹/₄	tsp
8	egg whites	8	
120 g	sugar	²/₃	cup
90 g	all-purpose flour	²/₃	cup
90 g	**oetker** Gustin corn starch	³/₄	cup

Batter:
PREHEAT oven to 230°C (450°F). Grease a 13 x 24 cm (5 x 9") loaf pan or a 23 cm (9") springform pan.
IN a mixing bowl, beat butter, icing sugar and marzipan until smooth and fluffy.
BEAT in egg yolks, vanilla sugar and allspice.
IN another bowl, beat egg whites and sugar to stiff peaks.
FOLD beaten egg whites into the butter mixture.
SIFT flour and corn starch over the butter mixture.
FOLD in gently but thoroughly.
POUR 125 mL (¹/₂ cup) of batter into prepared pan. Smooth surface.
BAKE on upper oven rack for 3 minutes.
BROIL for 1 minute or until top of cake is golden brown.
REMOVE from oven.
POUR another 125 mL (¹/₂ cup) of batter over top of the baked layer. Smooth surface.
BAKE for 3 minutes, broil for 1 minute.
REPEAT process until all the batter is used up.
COOL completely in the pan.
TURN onto a wire cooling rack.
USE as directed in recipes No. 684, 703, 716, and 725 or serve as is.

Cakes, Slices, Rolls

Pineapple-Raspberry Roll

Ananasstollen mit Himbeerrolle

Recipe No. 692

Batter:

4	eggs	4
80 g	sugar	$^1/_3$ cup
1 pkg	**oetker** vanilla sugar (9 g)	1 pkg
80 g	all-purpose flour	$^2/_3$ cup
5 mL	cocoa	1 tsp

Filling:

500 mL	whipping cream	2 cups
45 mL	sugar	3 tbsp
6 sheets	**oetker** gelatin sheets	6 sheets
50 mL	raspberries (fresh or frozen)	$^1/_4$ cup
75 mL	canned pineapple, crushed	$^1/_3$ cup
60 mL	pineapple juice juice of $^1/_2$ lemon	4 tbsp

Topping:

some	canned pineapple slices	some

Glaze:

1 pkg	**oetker** instant clear glaze (30 g)	1 pkg

Sprinkling:

some	chocolate sprinkles	some

Batter:

PREHEAT oven to 200°C (400°F). Line two 25 x 38 cm (10 x 15") baking sheets with waxed paper.

IN a mixing bowl, beat eggs, sugar and vanilla sugar until fluffy.

SIFT flour over the egg mixture. Fold in gently but thoroughly.

SPREAD two-thirds of the mixture $^1/_2$ cm ($^5/_8$") thick on one of the prepared baking sheets. (Batter may not cover entire baking sheet.)

ADD cocoa to the remaining mixture. Mix well.

SPREAD cocoa mixture $^1/_2$ cm ($^5/_8$") thick on the second prepared baking sheet. (Batter will not cover entire baking sheet.)

BAKE each pan, separately, for 10 minutes.

AFTER baking, remove light cake from pan immediately. Cool completely. Trim crisp edges from cake.

AFTER baking, turn dark cake out of pan onto a tea towel sprinkled generously with icing sugar.

TRIM crisp edges from cake.

BRUSH waxed paper with cold water and remove carefully but quickly.

ROLL up dark cake, using the towel.

Filling:

IN a mixing bowl, beat whipping cream and sugar to stiff peaks.

PREPARE gelatin according to package directions.

IN another bowl, crush raspberries.

STIR in 30 mL (2 tbsp) of gelatin and one-fifth of the whipped cream.

PLACE raspberry mixture in a pastry bag fitted with a large plain tube.

UNROLL dark cake. Pipe raspberry mixture down the centre of the cake.

FOLD cake so that the long ends meet. Wrap in tea towel and chill.

COMBINE pineapple, pineapple juice and lemon juice. Mix well.

ADD to remaining gelatin. (Gelatin may be reheated.)

FOLD pineapple mixture into remaining whipped cream.

REMOVE waxed paper from the light cake.

CUT and reserve one-third of the cake.

LINE a tube pan with the remaining two-thirds.

TURN one-third of the pineapple filling into the tube pan leaving a tunnel down the centre.

PLACE chilled raspberry roll in the tunnel.

TOP with reserved cake. Chill for 1 hour.

TURN roll onto a cake plate.

SPREAD remaining two-thirds of pineapple filling on the top and sides of the roll.

TOP with pineapple slices.

Glaze:

PREPARE glaze according to package directions.

SPOON carefully over pineapple slices.

GENTLY press chocolate sprinkles into the sides of the roll.

31

Apple-Quark Cake

Apfel-Topfenkuchen

Recipe No. 693

Dough:

250 g	all-purpose flour	1³/₄	cups
1 mL	**oetker** baking powder	¹/₄	tsp
100 g	icing sugar, sifted	³/₄	cup
1 pkg	**oetker** vanilla sugar (9 g)	1	pkg
pinch	salt		pinch
2 drops	**oetker** lemon flavouring concentrate	2	drops
150 g	butter, cold	²/₃	cup

Filling:

250 g	quark	1	cup
120 g	icing sugar, sifted	1	cup
1 pkg	**oetker** vanilla pudding (43 g)	1	pkg
¹/₂ btl	**oetker** lemon flavouring concentrate (1 mL)	¹/₂	btl
	juice of 1 lemon		
4	eggs	4	
250 mL	whipping cream	1	cup
2 pkgs	**oetker** vanilla sugar (18 g)	2	pkgs

Topping:

500 g	apples, peeled, cored and sliced	5	cups
45 mL	sugar	3	tbsp
2 mL	cinnamon	¹/₂	tsp

Glaze:

| 1 pkg | **oetker** instant clear glaze (30 g) | 1 | pkg |

Dough:
SIFT flour and baking powder onto a working surface.
MAKE a well in the centre. Put icing sugar, vanilla sugar, salt and flavouring concentrate in the well.
CUT butter into small pieces over the mixture.
COVER with flour.
STARTING from the centre, work ingredients into a smooth dough.
CHILL for 1 hour.
PREHEAT oven to 190°C (375°F).
PRESS two-thirds of the dough into the bottom of a 25 cm (10") springform pan.
PRESS remaining dough around the inside rim of the pan to form sides 3 cm (1¹/₄") high.

Filling:
IN a mixing bowl, beat quark, icing sugar, vanilla pudding, flavouring concentrate, lemon juice and eggs until smooth.
IN another bowl, beat whipping cream and vanilla sugar to a thick consistency.
FOLD into quark mixture gently but thoroughly.
TURN mixture into prepared pan.

Topping:
PLACE apple slices evenly over quark mixture.
MIX together sugar and cinnamon.
SPRINKLE over apple slices.
BAKE for 60-70 minutes.
REMOVE from pan. Cool completely.

Glaze:
PREPARE glaze according to package directions.
GLAZE cake.

Banana Roll

Bananenroulade

Recipe No. 694

Batter:

5	eggs	5
110 g	sugar	1/2 cup
1 pkg	**oetker** vanilla sugar (9 g)	1 pkg
130 g	all-purpose flour	1 cup
15 mL	cocoa	1 tbsp

Banana Cream Filling:

2	bananas	2
	juice of 1/2 lemon	
30 mL	rum	2 tbsp
3 sheets	**oetker** gelatin sheets	3 sheets
250 mL	whipping cream	1 cup

Dusting:

some	icing sugar, sifted	some

Batter:

PREHEAT oven to 200°C (400°F). Line a 28 x 43 cm (11 x 17") baking sheet with waxed paper.

IN a mixing bowl, beat eggs, sugar and vanilla sugar until thick and fluffy.

SIFT flour over egg mixture. Fold in gently but thoroughly.

PLACE one-half of the mixture in a pastry bag fitted with a round, plain tube.

PIPE mixture diagonally on prepared pan, 1 cm (3/8") apart. (If baking sheet has no rim, fold a piece of foil in place to prevent expanding dough from spilling in oven.)

ADD cocoa to remaining mixture.

PLACE cocoa mixture in a pastry bag fitted with a round, plain tube.

PIPE mixture in the spaces between the strips on the baking sheet.

BAKE for 10-12 minutes.

AFTER baking, turn cake onto a tea towel sprinkled generously with icing sugar.

TRIM crisp edges from cake.

BRUSH waxed paper with cold water. Remove paper carefully but quickly.

ROLL up cake using the tea towel. Chill.

Banana Cream:

PEEL and chop bananas. Place in a blender.

ADD lemon juice and rum. Puree.

PREPARE gelatin according to package directions.

IN a mixing bowl, beat whipping cream to stiff peaks.

FOLD pureed banana and gelatin into whipped cream gently but thoroughly. Chill.

UNROLL cake.

SPREAD cream evenly over surface of cake.

ROLL up cake.

DUST with icing sugar. Chill for 30 minutes.

Raspberry-Pineapple Bombe

Himbeer-Ananasbombe

Recipe No. 695

Batter:

4	eggs	4
80 g	sugar	1/3 cup
1 pkg	**oetker** vanilla sugar (9 g)	1 pkg
5 drops	**oetker** lemon flavour-ing concentrate	5 drops
80 g	all-purpose flour	2/3 cup
20 g	cocoa	1/4 cup

Raspberry Filling:

250 mL	raspberries, pureed	1 cup
1 pkg	**oetker** vanilla sugar (9 g)	1 pkg
60 g	icing sugar, sifted	1/2 cup
6 sheets	**oetker** gelatin sheets	6 sheets
250 mL	whipping cream	1 cup
1 can	pineapple pieces (540 mL/19 fl oz)	1 can

Bombe Filling:

250 mL	pineapple juice	1 cup
125 mL	white wine	1/2 cup
80 g	sugar	1/3 cup
	juice of 1 lemon	
1 pkg	**oetker** vanilla sugar (9 g)	1 pkg
6	**oetker** gelatin sheets	6
250 mL	whipping cream	1 cup

Glaze:

1 pkg	**oetker** instant clear glaze (30 g)	1 pkg

Decoration:

125 mL	whipped cream	1/2 cup

Batter:

PREHEAT oven to 200°C (400°F). Line a 25 x 38 cm (10 x 15") baking sheet with waxed paper.
IN a mixing bowl, beat eggs, sugar, vanilla sugar and flavouring concentrate until thick and fluffy.
MIX together flour and cocoa.
SIFT over egg mixture. Fold in gently but thoroughly.
SPREAD batter evenly into prepared pan. (If baking sheet has no rim, fold a piece of foil in place to prevent expanding dough from spilling in oven.)

BAKE for 10-12 minutes.
REMOVE cake from baking sheet immediately.
TRIM crisp edges from the cake. Cool completely. Remove waxed paper.
CUT into two 10 cm (4") wide strips.

Raspberry Filling:

IN a mixing bowl, combine pureed raspberries, vanilla sugar and icing sugar. Mix well.
PREPARE gelatin according to package directions.
FOLD into raspberry mixture gently but thoroughly. Chill.
BEAT whipping cream to stiff peaks.
WHEN raspberry mixture begins to set, fold in whipped cream.
PLACE mixture in a pastry bag fitted with a round plain tube.
PIPE mixture down the centre of each cake strip. Fold strips in half so ends meet.
WRAP in tea towel and chill for 1 hour.
LINE a bombe mold or a bowl with waxed paper.
SLICE raspberry rolls into 1 cm (3/8") pieces.
PLACE pieces of raspberry roll and pineapple alternately in the bottom and up the sides of the bombe mold or bowl. (Reserve some pineapple pieces for the bombe filling and raspberry roll pieces for the top of the bombe.)

Bombe Filling:

IN a mixing bowl, combine pineapple juice, wine, sugar, lemon juice, and vanilla sugar.
PREPARE gelatin according to package directions. Add to wine mixture.
IN a mixing bowl, beat whipping cream to stiff peaks.
WHEN gelatin mixture begins to set, fold in whipped cream and reserved pineapple pieces.
TURN filling into bombe mold or bowl. Top with reserved raspberry roll pieces.
CHILL for 2 hours.
LOOSEN bombe with a knife and by gently pulling on the waxed paper.
TURN bombe onto cake plate. Remove waxed paper.

Glaze:

PREPARE glaze according to package directions.
GLAZE bombe.
DECORATE with whipped cream.

Strawberry-Yogurt Roll

Erdbeer-Joghurtroulade

Recipe No. 696

Batter:

4	eggs	4
80 g	sugar	$^{1}/_{3}$ cup
1 pkg	**oetker** vanilla sugar (9 g)	1 pkg
5 drops	**oetker** lemon flavouring concentrate	5 drops
100 g	all-purpose flour	$^{3}/_{4}$ cup

Filling:

250 mL	yogurt	1 cup
80 g	icing sugar, sifted	$^{2}/_{3}$ cup
	juice of 1 lemon	
250 mL	strawberries, pureed	1 cup
6 sheets	**oetker** gelatin sheets	6 sheets
100 g	strawberries, chopped	$^{3}/_{4}$ cup
250 mL	whipping cream	1 cup

Decoration:

some	strawberries	some
some	pistachio nuts	some

Batter:

PREHEAT oven to 200°C (400°F). Line a 25 x 38 cm (10 x 15") baking sheet with waxed paper.

IN a mixing bowl, beat eggs, sugar, vanilla sugar and flavouring concentrate until thick and fluffy.

SIFT flour over egg mixture. Fold in gently but thoroughly.

SPREAD batter evenly into prepared pan. (If baking sheet has no rim, fold a piece of foil in place to prevent expanding dough from spilling in oven.)

BAKE for 10-12 minutes.

AFTER baking, turn cake out of pan onto a tea towel sprinkled generously with icing sugar.

TRIM crisp edges from cake.

BRUSH waxed paper with cold water.

REMOVE paper carefully but quickly.

ROLL up cake using the towel. Chill.

Filling:

IN a mixing bowl, combine yogurt, icing sugar, lemon juice and pureed strawberries.

MIX well.

PREPARE gelatin according to package directions.

FOLD gelatin into the yogurt mixture. Chill.

BEAT whipping cream to stiff peaks.

WHEN yogurt mixture begins to set, fold in strawberries and whipped cream gently but thoroughly.

UNROLL cake carefully.

SPREAD two-thirds of the filling over the surface of the cake. Roll up cake.

SPREAD remaining filling over surface and sides of the roll.

DECORATE with strawberries and pistachio nuts.

Snowcapped Apricot Flan

Marillenfleck mit Schneehaube

Recipe No. 697

Dough:

300	g	all-purpose flour	2 cups
1	pkg	**oetker** instant dry yeast (7 g)	1 pkg
	pinch	salt	pinch
1		egg yolk	1
80	g	sugar	$^1/_3$ cup
1	pkg	**oetker** vanilla sugar (9 g)	1 pkg
5	drops	**oetker** lemon flavour-ing concentrate	5 drops
50	mL	butter, melted	$^1/_4$ cup
250	mL	milk, lukewarm	1 cup

Topping:

1	kg	apricots, halved	6 cups
2	mL	cinnamon	$^1/_2$ tsp
45	mL	sugar	3 tbsp

Meringue:

4		egg whites	4
100	g	sugar	$^1/_2$ cup

Dough:

GREASE a 28 x 43 cm (11 x 17") baking sheet.
SIFT flour into a mixing bowl.
ADD yeast. Mix well.
MAKE a well in the centre. Put salt, egg yolk, sugar, vanilla sugar, flavouring concentrate, butter and milk in the well.
KNEAD with an electric mixer fitted with dough hooks on high speed until dough is smooth and no longer sticky (approximately 3 minutes).
SPREAD dough in prepared pan.
DISTRIBUTE apricots evenly over the dough.
MIX together cinnamon and sugar.
SPRINKLE over top of the apricots.
COVER and let rise in a warm place (approximately 15 minutes).
PREHEAT oven to 200°C (400°F).
BAKE for 20 minutes.

Meringue:

BEAT egg whites and sugar to stiff peaks.
PLACE beaten egg whites in a pastry bag fitted with a star tube.
PIPE decoratively over apricots. Return cake to oven.
BAKE for 5-7 minutes or until golden.
COOL completely.
CUT into serving pieces.

Blueberry Roll

Heidelbeerrolle

Recipe No. 698

Batter:

5	eggs	5
120 g	sugar	¹/₂ cup
1 pkg	**oetker** vanilla sugar (9 g)	1 pkg
¹/₂ btl	**oetker** lemon flavour-ing concentrate (1 mL)	¹/₂ btl
140 g	all-purpose flour	1¹/₄ cups

Filling:

125 g	cream cheese	¹/₂ cup
250 mL	whipping cream	1 cup
2 pkgs	**oetker** vanilla sugar (18 g)	2 pkgs
125 mL	blueberries, pureed	¹/₂ cup

Decoration:

250 mL	whipping cream	1 cup
50 g	icing sugar, sifted	¹/₃ cup
1 pkg	**oetker** Whip it (10 g)	1 pkg

Topping:

250 g	blueberries	2 cups

Glaze:

1 pkg	**oetker** instant clear glaze (30 g)	1 pkg

Batter:

PREHEAT oven to 200°C (400°F). Line a 28 x 43 cm (11 x 17") baking sheet with waxed paper.

IN a mixing bowl, beat eggs, sugar, vanilla sugar and flavouring concentrate until thick and fluffy.

SIFT flour over egg mixture. Fold in gently but thoroughly.

SPREAD batter evenly into prepared pan. (If baking sheet has no rim, fold a piece of foil in place to prevent expanding dough from spilling in oven.)

BAKE for 12-15 minutes.

AFTER baking, turn cake onto a tea towel sprinkled generously with icing sugar.

TRIM crisp edges from cake.

BRUSH waxed paper with cold water. Remove carefully but quickly.

ROLL up cake using the towel.

Filling:

IN a mixing bowl, beat cream cheese until smooth.

IN another bowl, beat whipping cream and vanilla sugar to stiff peaks.

FOLD whipped cream into the cream cheese gently but thoroughly. Stir in pureed blueberries.

UNROLL cake carefully. Spread cream evenly over the surface of the cake.

ROLL up cake.

Decoration:

IN a mixing bowl, beat whipping cream, icing sugar and Whip it to stiff peaks.

PLACE whipped cream in a pastry bag fitted with a star tube.

DECORATIVELY pipe whipped cream on the top and sides of the cake.

TOP with blueberries. (When using frozen blueberries, do not thaw.)

Glaze:

PREPARE glaze according to package directions. Cool slightly.

SPOON over blueberries.

Poppyseed Cake

Mohnputize

Recipe No. 699

Dough:

250 g	all-purpose flour	1³/₄ cups
1 pkg	**oetker** instant dry yeast (7 g)	1 pkg
80 g	sugar	¹/₄ cup
2 pkgs	**oetker** vanilla sugar (18 g)	2 pkgs
110 g	butter, softened	¹/₂ cup
125 g	quark, room temperature	¹/₂ cup
2	eggs	2
125 mL	milk, lukewarm	¹/₂ cup
pinch	salt	pinch
15 mL	rum	1 tbsp
¹/₂ btl	**oetker** rum flavouring concentrate (1 mL)	¹/₂ btl
¹/₂ btl	**oetker** lemon flavouring concentrate (1 mL)	¹/₂ btl
60 g	almonds, sliced	³/₄ cup

Filling:

175 mL	milk	³/₄ cup
100 g	sugar	¹/₃ cup
310 g	poppy seeds, ground	3¹/₄ cups
1 pkg	**oetker** vanilla sugar (9 g)	1 pkg
¹/₂ btl	**oetker** rum flavouring concentrate (1 mL)	¹/₂ btl
100 g	raisins	³/₄ cup
2	eggs	2

Topping:

1 can	pear pieces (540 mL/19 fl oz)	1 can

Dusting:

some	icing sugar, sifted	some

Dough:

GREASE two 22 cm (9") loaf pans.
IN a mixing bowl, combine flour and yeast.
MIX well.
MAKE a well in the centre. Put sugar, vanilla sugar, butter, quark, eggs, milk, salt, rum, flavouring concentrates and almonds in the well.
USING an electric mixer with dough hook attachments, knead dough until smooth.
LET rest until doubled in size.
PREHEAT oven to 180°C (350°F).

Filling:

IN a saucepan, bring milk and sugar to a boil.
ADD poppy seeds, vanilla sugar, flavouring concentrate and raisins. Cool slightly.
FOLD in eggs gently but thoroughly.
ROLL dough into a 30 x 45 cm (12 x 18") rectangle, ¹/₂ cm (⁵/₈") thick.
DIVIDE the dough in half.
SPREAD poppy seed mixture evenly over the surface of each half.
DISTRIBUTE pear pieces evenly over poppy seed mixture.
ROLL up dough, at both ends, so that the rolls meet in the centre.
PLACE in prepared pans.
BAKE for 60-70 minutes.
AFTER baking, cool in pan.
TURN onto wire cooling racks.
DUST with icing sugar.

Raspberry Cake

Himbeerkuchen

Recipe No. 700

Batter:

3	eggs	3
80 g	sugar	$^1/_3$ cup
1 pkg	**oetker** vanilla sugar (9 g)	1 pkg
3 drops	**oetker** lemon flavouring concentrate	3 drops
80 g	all-purpose flour	$^1/_2$ cup

Filling:

150 mL	raspberry jam	$^2/_3$ cup

Sponge Cake:

110 g	butter or margarine	$^1/_2$ cup
100 g	icing sugar, sifted	$^3/_4$ cup
1 pkg	**oetker** vanilla sugar (9 g)	1 pkg
5 drops	**oetker** lemon flavouring concentrate	5 drops
2	eggs	2
200 g	all-purpose flour	$1^1/_2$ cups
$^1/_2$ pkg	**oetker** baking powder (7 g)	$^1/_2$ pkg
125 mL	milk	$^1/_2$ cup

Spreading and Topping:

30 mL	raspberry jam	2 tbsp
250 g	raspberries	2 cups

Glaze:

1 pkg	**oetker** instant clear glaze (30 g)	1 pkg

Batter:

PREHEAT oven to 200°C (400°F). Line a 28 x 43 cm (11 x 17") baking sheet with waxed paper.

IN a mixing bowl, beat eggs, sugar, vanilla sugar and flavouring concentrate until thick and fluffy.

SIFT flour over the egg mixture. Fold in gently but thoroughly.

TURN batter into prepared pan. (If baking sheet has no rim, fold a piece of foil in place to prevent expanding dough from spilling in oven.)

BAKE for 10 minutes.

AFTER baking, turn cake onto a tea towel sprinkled generously with icing sugar.

BRUSH waxed paper with cold water. Remove carefully but quickly.

TRIM crisp edges from cake.

HEAT jam. Spread jam over surface of cake.

ROLL up cake, from the long side, using the towel.

Sponge Cake:

PREHEAT oven to 180°C (350°F). Grease a 23 cm (9") loaf pan. Dust lightly with flour.

IN a mixing bowl, beat butter, icing sugar, vanilla sugar and flavouring concentrate until fluffy.

ADD eggs, one at a time, beating after each addition.

SIFT together flour and baking powder.

STIR into the butter mixture alternately with milk.

TURN one-half of the batter into the prepared pan.

PLACE prepared jelly roll on top of the batter.

FILL pan with remaining batter.

BAKE for 35 minutes.

REMOVE from pan. Turn onto a wire cooling rack. Cool completely.

SPREAD jam over the surface of the cake. Top with raspberries.

Glaze:

PREPARE glaze according to package directions.

SPOON glaze over raspberries.

47

*W*ine Delight

*W*inzerinterrine

Recipe No. 701

Batter:

3	eggs	3
60 g	icing sugar, sifted	½ cup
1 pkg	**oetker** vanilla sugar (9 g)	1 pkg
60 g	all-purpose flour	½ cup
15 mL	cocoa	1 tbsp

Filling:

250 mL	Marsala wine	1 cup
80 g	sugar	⅓ cup
1 pkg	**oetker** vanilla sugar (9 g)	1 pkg
2	egg yolks	2
6 sheets	**oetker** gelatin sheets	6 sheets
250 mL	whipping cream	1 cup

Decoration:

some	white grapes, blue grapes, honey, brandy	some

Batter:

PREHEAT oven to 200°C (400°F). Line a 25 x 38 cm (10 x 15") baking sheet with waxed paper.

IN a mixing bowl, beat eggs, icing sugar and vanilla sugar until thick and fluffy.

MIX together flour and cocoa.

SIFT over egg mixture. Fold in gently but thoroughly.

TURN batter into prepared pan. (If baking sheet has no rim, fold a piece of foil in place to prevent expanding dough from spilling in oven.)

BAKE for 8-10 minutes.

TURN cake onto a tea towel sprinkled generously with icing sugar.

BRUSH waxed paper with cold water. Remove carefully but quickly.

TRIM crisp edges from cake, cut into cubes and reserve.

LINE a tube pan with two-thirds of the cake.

RESERVE the remaining one-third for a lid.

Filling:

IN a double boiler, combine wine, sugar, vanilla sugar and egg yolks.

HEAT to a temperature of 60°C (125°F), stirring constantly.

PREPARE gelatin according to package directions.

STIR into the wine mixture. Let cool.

IN a mixing bowl, beat whipping cream to stiff peaks.

WHEN wine mixture begins to set, fold in whipped cream and reserved cake cubes.

TURN whipped cream mixture into the tube pan. Top with cake lid. Chill for 2-3 hours.

DIP pan quickly in hot water. Turn onto a cake plate.

DECORATE with grapes.

Tip: Halve grapes. Remove seeds. Add honey and brandy to taste.

Blackberry Strudel

Schwarzbeerstrudel

Recipe No. 702

Dough:
1 pkg	frozen puff pastry dough	1	pkg

Filling:
500 g	quark	2	cups
60 mL	honey	4	tbsp
2	eggs	2	
1 pkg	**oetker** vanilla sugar (9 g)	1	pkg
pinch	salt		pinch
250 g	blackberries (fresh or frozen)	2	cups

Brushing:
1	egg	1	
15 mL	milk	1	tbsp

Dough:
PREHEAT oven to 200°C (400°F). Grease a baking sheet.
THAW puff pastry according to package directions.
ROLL pastry into two 30 x 30 cm (12 x 12") squares.

Filling:
IN a mixing bowl, beat quark, honey, eggs, vanilla sugar and salt.
SPREAD mixture in the centre of each square.
DISTRIBUTE blackberries evenly over the quark mixture.
FOLD dough so that the ends meet.
PLACE the dough, seam side up, onto prepared baking sheet.
WHISK together egg and milk.
BRUSH each roll with the egg mixture.
BAKE 35 minutes.

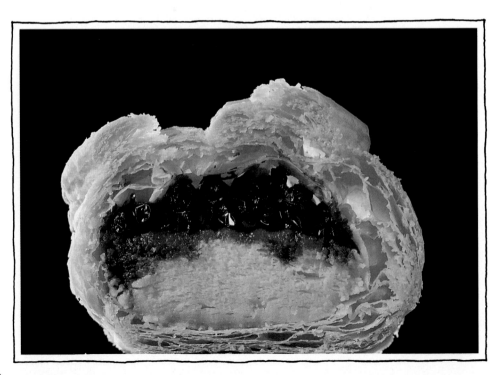

Yogurt-Strawberry Roll

Joghurt-Erdbeerterrine

Recipe No. 703

Batter:
Marzipan Layer Cake
(See Recipe No. 691)

Filling:

250 mL	yogurt	1	cup
150 g	icing sugar, sifted	1½	cups
1 pkg	**oetker** vanilla sugar (9 g)	1	pkg
3 drops	**oetker** lemon flavouring concentrate	3	drops
	juice of 1 lemon		
12 sheets	**oetker** gelatin sheets	12	sheets
250 mL	strawberries, pureed	1	cup
some	strawberries		some

Strawberry Sauce:

250 g	strawberries	2½	cups
75 g	icing sugar, sifted	⅔	cup
1 pkg	**oetker** vanilla sugar (9 g)	1	pkg

Decoration:

some	yogurt	some

Batter:

PREPARE marzipan layer cake as directed on page 27.
LINE a tube pan with slices of the baked layer cake, 3 mm (⅛") thick.
CUT a piece of cake to serve as a lid.

Filling:

IN a mixing bowl, combine yogurt, icing sugar, vanilla sugar, flavouring concentrate and lemon juice. Mix well.
PREPARE gelatin according to package directions.
FOLD into the pureed strawberries gently but thoroughly.
FOLD strawberry mixture into the yogurt mixture. Chill.
WHEN the mixture begins to set, spoon into prepared pan.
SET strawberries in the mixture. Cover with cake lid. Chill for 2 hours.

Strawberry Sauce:

IN a blender, puree strawberries, icing sugar and vanilla sugar.
DIP tube pan in hot water. Turn onto a dessert platter.
SERVE slices of cake with strawberry sauce and yogurt.

51

Quark-Apricot Strudel with Yogurt Sauce

Topfen-Marillenstrudel mit Joghurtsoße

Recipe No. 704

Dough:

1 pkg	frozen puff pastry dough	1	pkg

Filling:

50 g	butter, softened	1/4	cup
30 g	icing sugar, sifted	1/4	cup
1 mL	salt	1/4	tsp
1 pkg	**oetker** vanilla sugar (9 g)	1	pkg
1/2 btl	**oetker** lemon flavour-ing concentrate (1 mL)	1/2	btl
2	egg yolks	2	
2	bread rolls, crust removed	2	
125 mL	milk	1/2	cup
375 g	cream cheese	1 1/2	cups
125 mL	whipping cream	1/2	cup
2	egg whites	2	
60 g	sugar	1/4	cup
250 g	apricots, halved	1	cup

Brushing:

some	melted better		some

Sauce:

500 mL	yogurt	2	cups
80 g	icing sugar, sifted	2/3	cup
1 pkg	**oetker** vanilla sugar (9 g)	1	pkg
some	cassis liqueur (black currant)		some

Dough:

PREHEAT oven to 200°C (400°F). Grease two baking sheets.

THAW puff pastry according to package directions.

ROLL pastry into two 30 x 30 cm (12 x 12") squares. Place on baking sheets.

Filling:

IN a mixing bowl, beat butter, icing sugar, salt, vanilla sugar and flavouring concentrate until fluffy.

ADD egg yolks, one at a time, mixing well after each addition.

SOAK the rolls in milk. Squeeze out excess moisture.

ADD to the butter mixture.

IN another bowl, beat cream cheese until smooth.

ADD cream cheese and whipping cream to the egg mixture. Mix well.

BEAT egg whites and sugar to stiff peaks.

SPOON beaten egg whites over the cream cheese mixture. Fold in gently but thoroughly.

DIVIDE filling in half.

SPREAD one half of the filling over two-thirds of one of the squares. Top with half of the apricot halves. Repeat with remaining square.

ROLL up squares, starting from the end with the filling.

BRUSH with melted butter.

BAKE for 30-35 minutes or until golden brown.

Sauce:

IN a mixing bowl, combine yogurt, icing sugar and vanilla sugar.

POUR onto dessert plates. Pour a small amount of cassis in the centre.

USING a toothpick, swirl the sauce.

SERVE with strudel.

53

Rhubarb Surprise

Rhabarberterrine

Recipe No. 705

Batter:

3	eggs	3
80 g	sugar	$^1/_3$ cup
$^1/_2$ pkg	**oetker** vanilla sugar (4.5 g)	$^1/_2$ pkg
90 g	all-purpose flour	$^2/_3$ cup

Filling:

600 g	rhubarb	$3^1/_2$ cups
250 g	sugar	$1^1/_4$ cups
1 pkg	**oetker** vanilla sugar (9 g)	1 pkg
5 drops	**oetker** lemon flavouring concentrate	5 drops
30 mL	lemon juice	2 tbsp
1 mL	cinnamon	$^1/_4$ tsp
60 mL	kirsch (cherry brandy)	4 tbsp
10 sheets	**oetker** gelatin sheets	10 sheets
500 mL	whipping cream	2 cups

Topping:

2	egg whites	2
30 mL	sugar	2 tbsp

Batter:

PREHEAT oven to 200°C (400°F). Line a 25 x 38 cm (10 x 15") baking sheet with waxed paper.

IN a mixing bowl, beat eggs, sugar and vanilla sugar until thick and fluffy.

SIFT flour over egg mixture. Fold in gently but thoroughly.

TURN batter into prepared baking sheet. (If baking sheet has no rim, fold a piece of foil in place to prevent expanding dough from spilling in oven.)

BAKE for 8 minutes.

AFTER baking, turn cake onto a tea towel sprinkled generously with icing sugar.

BRUSH waxed paper with cold water. Remove quickly but carefully. Let cake cool completely. TRIM crisp edges from cake.

LINE a tube pan with two-thirds of the cake. RESERVE remaining one-third for a lid.

Filling:

PEEL rhubarb and cut into 5 cm (2") pieces. SPRINKLE with sugar and vanilla sugar. Mix well.

COVER. Marinate for 20 minutes.

STEAM until soft.

PUREE two-thirds of the rhubarb. Set aside remaining one-third.

ADD flavouring concentrate, lemon juice, cinnamon and kirsch to the pureed rhubarb. PREPARE gelatin according to package directions.

FOLD into rhubarb mixture gently but thoroughly. Chill.

IN another bowl, beat whipping cream to stiff peaks.

WHEN mixture begins to set, add whipped cream and reserved rhubarb.

TURN rhubarb mixture into the pan. Top with reserved cake strip.

CHILL for 2-3 hours.

Optional Meringue Topping:

PREHEAT oven to 220°C (425°F).

BEAT egg whites and sugar to stiff peaks.

PLACE beaten egg white in a pastry bag fitted with a medium star tube.

TURN cake onto baking sheet.

DECORATE with egg white mixture, as desired.

BAKE on middle oven rack for 3 minutes.

REFRIGERATE immediately.

Lemon-Yogurt Roll

Zitronen(Joghurt-)rolle

Recipe No. 706

Batter:

6	egg yolks	6
80 g	sugar	$^1/_3$ cup
1 pkg	**oetker** vanilla sugar (9 g)	1 pkg
5 drops	**oetker** lemon flavour-ing concentrate	5 drops
4	egg whites	4
40 g	all-purpose flour	$^1/_4$ cup
40 g	**oetker** Gustin corn starch	$^1/_3$ cup

Filling:

250 mL	yogurt	1 cup
80 g	icing sugar, sifted	$^2/_3$ cup
	juice of 1 lemon	
$^1/_2$ btl	**oetker** lemon flavour-ing concentrate (1 mL)	$^1/_2$ btl
1 pkg	**oetker** vanilla sugar (9 g)	1 pkg
6 sheets	**oetker** gelatin sheets	6 sheets
250 mL	whipping cream	1 cup

Glaze:

1 pkg	**oetker** instant clear glaze (30 g)	1 pkg

Decoration:

some	lemon slices	some

Batter:

PREHEAT oven to 220°C (425°F). Line a 25 x 38 cm (10 x 15") baking sheet with waxed paper.

IN a mixing bowl, beat egg yolks, one-half of the sugar, vanilla sugar and flavouring concentrate until thick and fluffy.

IN another bowl, beat egg whites and remaining sugar to stiff peaks.

FOLD beaten egg whites into the egg yolk mixture.

COMBINE flour and corn starch. Sift over the egg mixture.

FOLD in gently but thoroughly.

TURN batter into prepared baking sheet. (If baking sheet has no rim, fold a piece of foil in place to prevent expanding dough from spilling in oven.)

BAKE for 10 minutes.

AFTER baking, turn cake onto a tea towel sprinkled generously with icing sugar.

BRUSH the waxed paper with cold water.

REMOVE quickly but carefully.

TRIM crisp edges from cake.

ROLL up cake using the towel.

Filling:

IN a mixing bowl, combine yogurt, icing sugar, lemon juice, flavouring concentrate and vanilla sugar. Mix well.

PREPARE gelatin according to package directions.

FOLD into the yogurt mixture gently but thoroughly. Chill.

IN another bowl, beat whipping cream to stiff peaks.

WHEN the gelatin mixture begins to set, fold in whipped cream.

ROLL out cake carefully. Spread cream down the centre of the cake. Fold cake so that the ends meet. Wrap in tea towel.

CHILL for one hour. Cut into 15 cm (6") long slices.

Glaze:

PREPARE glaze according to package directions.

GLAZE each slice.

DECORATE with lemon slices.

Pastries

Pineapple Windows

Ananas im Fenster

Recipe No. 707

Dough:

1 pkg	frozen puff pastry dough	1	pkg
30 mL	sugar	2	tbsp

Filling:

250 g	cream cheese	1	cup
1	egg yolk	1	
1 pkg	**oetker** vanilla pudding (43 g)	1	pkg
80 g	icing sugar, sifted	$^2/_3$	cup
5 drops	**oetker** lemon flavouring concentrate	5	drops
10 slices	pineapple, halved	10	slices

Brushing and Glazing:

1	egg white, beaten	1	
1 pkg	**oetker** instant clear glaze (30 g)	1	pkg

Dough:
PREHEAT oven to 200°C (400°F).
THAW puff pastry according to package directions.
SPRINKLE a working surface with sugar.
ROLL out dough thinly.
USING a knife, cut out 10 cm (4") squares.
CUT windows out of each square. Fold dough over the window (see photo).
PLACE dough on baking sheet.

Filling:
IN a mixing bowl, beat cream cheese, egg yolk, pudding, icing sugar and flavouring concentrate until smooth.
FILL each window with cream cheese mixture.
TOP with pineapple slice.
BRUSH dough lightly with beaten egg white.
BAKE for 15-18 minutes.
COOL completely.

Glaze:
PREPARE glaze according to package directions.
GLAZE each pineapple slice.

Berry Bavarian Pastries

Bayrische Kniekūchlein

Recipe No. 708

Dough:

500	g	all-purpose flour	3¹/₂ cups
1	pkg	**oetker** instant dry yeast (7 g)	1 pkg
	pinch	salt	pinch
120	g	sugar	¹/₂ cup
1	pkg	**oetker** vanilla sugar (9 g)	1 pkg
15	mL	rum	1 tbsp
¹/₂	btl	**oetker** lemon flavouring concentrate (1 mL)	¹/₂ btl
4		egg yolks	4
75	mL	butter, melted	¹/₃ cup
250	mL	milk, lukewarm	1 cup

Deep Frying:

vegetable oil

Filling:

cranberry sauce

Dusting:

some	icing sugar, sifted		some
1	pkg	**oetker** vanilla sugar (9 g)	1 pkg

Dough:

SIFT flour into a mixing bowl.
SPRINKLE yeast over the flour. Mix well.
MAKE a well in the centre. Put salt, sugar, vanilla sugar, rum, flavouring concentrate, egg yolks, butter and milk in the well.
KNEAD dough with an electric mixer fitted with dough hooks on high speed until dough is smooth, blistery and no longer sticky.
COVER. Let rest in a warm place until doubled in size.
CUT off pieces and shape into small balls. Using your thumb, make a small well in the centre.
PLACE balls on a towel sprinkled with flour.
COVER. Let rest, until doubled in size.
PULL dough gently from all sides until the dough is notably thin in the centre.
FILL a deep fryer half way with vegetable oil.
HEAT slowly. During the frying process, the temperature should be kept at a constant, 180°C (350°F). Place dough in hot oil.
DEEP fry until golden brown.
REMOVE from oil using a slotted spoon.
DRAIN on paper towels.
FILL centres with cranberry sauce.
DUST with icing sugar and vanilla sugar.

Pineapple Tartlets

Ananastörtchen

Recipe No. 709

Dough:

280 g	all-purpose flour	2	cups
80 g	icing sugar, sifted	²/₃	cup
1 pkg	**oetker** vanilla sugar (9 g)	1	pkg
5 drops	**oetker** lemon flavouring concentrate	5	drops
1	egg yolk	1	
180 g	butter, cold	³/₄	cup

Cream Filling:

2 pkgs	**oetker** vanilla pudding (86 g)	2	pkgs
500 mL	milk	2	cups
5 drops	**oetker** rum flavouring concentrate	5	drops
2	egg yolks	2	
3	egg whites	3	
80 g	sugar	¹/₃	cup

Topping:

20 slices	pineapple, halved, drained	20	slices
50 mL	raspberry jam	¹/₄	cup

Glaze:

1 pkg	**oetker** instant clear glaze (30 g)	1	pkg

Dough:

GREASE tartlet tins.
SIFT flour onto a working surface.
MAKE a well in the centre. Put icing sugar, vanilla sugar, flavouring concentrate and egg yolk in the well.
CUT butter in small pieces over the flour mixture.
COVER with flour.
STARTING from the centre, work ingredients into a smooth dough. Chill for 30 minutes.
PREHEAT oven to 180°C (350°F).
ROLL out dough thinly.
LINE each tartlet tin with dough.
BAKE for 14 minutes.

Cream Filling:

IN a mixing bowl, combine pudding with a small amount of milk, flavouring concentrate and egg yolks. Mix well.
IN a saucepan, over medium heat, bring remaining milk to a boil.
REMOVE from heat and stir in pudding mixture.
BRING to a full boil again over medium heat, stirring constantly until smoothly thickened.
REMOVE from heat.
IN another bowl, beat egg whites and sugar to stiff peaks.
FOLD beaten egg whites into the hot pudding mixture gently but thoroughly. Let cool.
PLACE pudding mixture in a pastry bag fitted with a large star tube.
PIPE mixture into baked tartlets.
TOP with pineapple halves and raspberry jam.

Glaze:

PREPARE glaze according to package directions.
GLAZE tartlets.

Apricot Puffs

Elsässer Marillenkrapfen

Recipe No. 710

Dough:

250	mL	water	1 cup
110	g	butter	$^1/_2$ cup
1	mL	salt	$^1/_4$ tsp
135	g	all-purpose flour	1 cup
4-5		eggs	4-5

Brushing:

1	egg yolk, beaten	1

Sprinkling:

some	coarse sugar crystals	some

Filling:

1	can	apricot halves, drained (540 mL/19 fl oz)	1 can
250	mL	whipping cream	1 cup
1	pkg	**oetker** Whip it (10 g)	1 pkg

Sauce:

250	mL	apricot juice	1 cup
15	mL	**oetker** Gustin corn starch	1 tbsp
	some	apricot liqueur	some

Dough:

IN a saucepan, bring water, butter and salt to a boil.

REMOVE from heat and add flour all at once.

STIR over medium heat until mixture forms a ball around the spoon and pulls away from the side of the pan. (Do not overcook.) Cool slightly.

ADD unbeaten eggs to dough one at a time, stirring thoroughly after each addition until smooth. Continue stirring until mixture is shiny and no longer sticky.

CHILL until mixture holds its shape.

PREHEAT oven to 200°C (400°F).

PLACE dough in a pastry bag fitted with a large plain tube.

PIPE balls, the size of a small tangerine, onto an ungreased baking sheet.

BRUSH balls with beaten egg yolk. Sprinkle with sugar crystals.

BAKE for 25-30 minutes. (Do not open oven door during the first 15 minutes of baking, pastry may collapse.)

REMOVE puffs from baking sheet. Cool completely.

SLICE each puff in half.

Filling:

PLACE an apricot on each bottom half.

IN a mixing bowl, beat whipping cream and Whip it to stiff peaks.

SPOON whipped cream over apricots.

COVER with top half.

Sauce:

IN a saucepan, combine apricot juice and corn starch. Bring to a boil. Cool.

STIR in apricot liqueur, to taste.

BRUSH pastries with apricot mixture.

Chocolate-Topped Melon Cream

Melonentimbal mit Schokofülle

Recipe No. 711

Batter:

4	eggs	4
80 g	sugar	$^1/_3$ cup
1 pkg	**oetker** vanilla sugar (9 g)	1 pkg
$^1/_2$ btl	**oetker** lemon flavouring concentrate (1 mL)	$^1/_2$ btl
80 g	all-purpose flour	$^2/_3$ cup
15 mL	cocoa	1 tbsp

Spreading:

250 mL	cherry jam	1 cup

Melon Cream:

$^1/_2$	honeydew melon	$^1/_2$
50 g	sugar	$^1/_4$ cup
1 pkg	**oetker** vanilla sugar (9 g)	1 pkg
30 mL	rum	2 tbsp
pinch	cinnamon	pinch
10 sheets	**oetker** gelatin sheets	10 sheets
500 mL	whipping cream	2 cups
50 g	milk chocolate, melted	3 squares

Decoration:

$^1/_2$	honeydew melon, cubed	$^1/_2$
some	Grand Marnier	some
125 mL	whipped cream	$^1/_2$ cup
some	milk chocolate, shaved	some

Batter:

PREHEAT oven to 200°C (400°F). Line a 25 x 38 cm (10 x 15") baking sheet with waxed paper.

IN a mixing bowl, beat eggs, sugar, vanilla sugar and flavouring concentrate until thick and fluffy.

MIX together flour and cocoa.

SIFT over egg mixture. Fold in gently but thoroughly.

TURN mixture into prepared baking sheet.

BAKE for 10-12 minutes.

AFTER baking, turn cake onto a tea towel sprinkled generously with icing sugar.

BRUSH waxed paper with cold water. Remove quickly but carefully.

TRIM crisp edges from cake.

SPREAD jam over surface of cake.

ROLL up cake, from the long side, using the tea towel. Chill.

CUT cake into 1 cm ($^3/_8$") thick slices.

PLACE each slice into small timbale pans. (Muffin tins may be used if timbale pans are not available.)

Melon Cream:

PEEL, seed and chop melon into small pieces.

IN a blender, puree melon pieces, sugar, vanilla sugar, rum and cinnamon.

PREPARE gelatin according to package directions.

STIR into the pureed melon. Chill.

IN a mixing bowl, beat whipping cream to stiff peaks.

WHEN the melon cream begins to set, fold in whipped cream gently but thoroughly.

FILL pans or tins with two-thirds of the melon cream.

STIR melted chocolate into the remaining cream.

POUR chocolate cream over melon cream in pans or tins.

CHILL for 2-3 hours.

DIP pans or tins quickly in hot water. Loosen edges and turn onto a baking sheet.

TRANSFER to dessert plates.

DRIZZLE melon cubes with Grand Marnier.

SERVE melon cubes, whipped cream and chocolate shavings with dessert.

Quark Cream Puffs

Topfenwindbeutel

Recipe No. 712

Dough:

250 mL	water	1	cup
110 g	butter	½	cup
1 mL	salt	¼	tsp
pinch	sugar		pinch
135 g	all-purpose flour	1	cup
4	eggs	4	

Filling:

250 mL	whipping cream	1	cup
350 g	quark	1⅓	cups
2 pkgs	**oetker** vanilla sugar (18 g)	2	pkgs

Dusting:

some	icing sugar, sifted	some	

Decoration:

	assorted fruits

Dough:
PREHEAT oven to 200°C (400°F).
IN a saucepan, bring water, butter, salt and sugar to a boil.
REMOVE from heat and add flour all at once.
STIR constantly over medium heat until mixture forms a ball around the spoon and pulls away from the side of the pan (approximately 1 minute). Do not overcook.
PLACE hot dough in a mixing bowl, cool slightly. Add unbeaten eggs to the dough one at a time, stirring after each addition. Beat mixture until shiny and no longer sticky.
CHILL until mixture holds its shape.
PLACE dough in a pastry bag fitted with a large star tube.
SQUEEZE circles, 8 cm (3") in diameter, onto an ungreased baking sheet.
BAKE for 25 minutes. (Do not open oven door during the first 15 minutes of baking, pastry may collapse.)
WHILE pastry is warm, cut in half.

Filling:
BEAT whipping cream to stiff peaks. Fold in quark and vanilla sugar. Stir until smooth.
FILL bottom half of puff with quark mixture.
COVER with top half.
DUST with icing sugar. Decorate with fruits.

69

Mini Mascarpone Layer Cakes

Mascarpone-Torteletts

Recipe No. 713

Batter:

5	eggs	5
140 g	sugar	²/₃ cup
1 pkg	**oetker** vanilla sugar (9 g)	1 pkg
5 drops	**oetker** lemon flavouring concentrate	5 drops
120 g	all-purpose flour	1 cup

Cream:

300 g	Mascarpone cheese	1¹/₃ cups
5	egg yolks	5
30 mL	whipping cream	2 tbsp
30 mL	rum	2 tbsp
1 pkg	**oetker** vanilla sugar (9 g)	1 pkg
4	egg whites	4
100 g	icing sugar, sifted	³/₄ cup

Dipping:

250 mL	strong black coffee	1 cup
1 pkg	**oetker** vanilla sugar (9 g)	1 pkg

Dusting:

some	cocoa	some

Coffee Sauce:

250 mL	milk	1 cup
250 mL	whipping cream	1 cup
120 g	sugar	²/₃ cup
10 mL	instant coffee	2 tsp
3	egg yolks	3
30 mL	**oetker** vanilla pudding	2 tbsp

Batter:

PREHEAT oven to 200°C (400°F). Lightly grease muffin tins.

IN a mixing bowl, beat eggs, sugar, vanilla sugar and flavouring concentrate until thick and fluffy.

SIFT flour over egg mixture. Fold in gently but thoroughly.

TURN 30 mL (2 tbsp) of batter into each muffin cup.

BAKE for 10-12 minutes. Cool in tins.

REMOVE slices. Set aside.

Cream:

IN a mixing bowl, beat Mascarpone cheese, egg yolks, whipping cream, rum and vanilla sugar until thick and fluffy.

IN another bowl, beat egg whites and icing sugar to stiff peaks.

FOLD beaten egg whites into cheese mixture gently but thoroughly.

Dipping:

COMBINE coffee and vanilla sugar.

DIP each slice in the mixture.

PIPE cream on the surface of three slices and sandwich together. (See photo.)

DUST surface of layer cake with cocoa. Chill for 2-3 hours.

Coffee Sauce:

IN a saucepan, combine milk, whipping cream, sugar, instant coffee, egg yolks and pudding.

BRING mixture to a boil, over medium heat, stirring constantly. Let cool.

SERVE sauce with mini layer cakes.

71

Peach-Cranberry Tartlets

Pfirsich-Preiselbeertörtchen

Recipe No. 714

Dough:

280 g	all-purpose flour	2 cups
100 g	icing sugar, sifted	³/₄ cup
1 pkg	**oetker** vanilla sugar (9 g)	1 pkg
pinch	salt	pinch
¹/₂ btl	**oetker** lemon flavouring concentrate (1 mL)	¹/₂ btl
180 g	butter, cold	³/₄ cup

Cream Filling:

250 mL	milk	1 cup
2	egg yolks	2
100 g	sugar	¹/₂ cup
1 pkg	**oetker** vanilla sugar (9 g)	1 pkg
¹/₂ btl	**oetker** lemon flavouring concentrate (1 mL)	¹/₂ btl
6 sheets	**oetker** gelatin sheets	6 sheets
250 mL	whipping cream	1 cup
250 g	quark	1 cup
	juice of ¹/₂ lemon	

Topping:

4-5 cans	peach halves (398 mL/14 fl oz)	4-5 cans
1 can	cranberry sauce (398 mL/14 fl oz)	1 can

Dough:

GREASE several small tartlet pans. Dust lightly with flour.
SIFT flour onto a working surface.
MAKE a well in the centre. Put icing sugar, vanilla sugar, salt and flavouring concentrate in the well.
CUT butter in small pieces over the mixture.
COVER with flour.
STARTING from the centre, work ingredients into a smooth dough. Chill.
PREHEAT oven to 180°C (350°F).
ROLL out dough thinly.
LINE prepared pans with dough. Prick dough with fork.
BAKE for 10-12 minutes.
COOL completely. Remove from tins.

Cream Filling:

IN a saucepan, combine milk, egg yolks, sugar, vanilla sugar and flavouring concentrate.
STIRRING constantly, heat to a temperature of 80°C (150°F). Remove from heat.
PREPARE gelatin according to package directions.
STIR into hot milk mixture. Cool completely.
IN a mixing bowl, beat whipping cream to stiff peaks.
WHEN gelatin mixture begins to set, fold in whipped cream, quark and lemon juice gently but thoroughly.
SPOON cream into baked tartlets.
TOP with a peach half. Decorate with cranberry sauce.
CHILL for 2-3 hours.

Apricot Bread Ring

Marillen à la Prälat Savarin

Recipe No. 715

Dough:

250 g	all-purpose flour	1³/₄	cups
1 pkg	**oetker** instant dry yeast (7 g)	1	pkg
pinch	salt		pinch
2	egg yolks	2	
50 g	sugar	¹/₄	cup
1 pkg	**oetker** vanilla sugar (9 g)	1	pkg
2 drops	**oetker** lemon flavour-ing concentrate	2	drops
30 mL	butter, melted	2	tbsp
125 mL	milk, lukewarm	¹/₂	cup

Topping:

2 cans	apricot halves (398 mL/14 fl oz)	2	cans
some	kirsch (cherry brandy)		some
some	icing sugar, sifted		some

Cherry Cream Sauce:

2	egg yolks	2	
100 g	icing sugar, sifted	³/₄	cup
	peel of ¹/₂ orange		
125 mL	whipping cream	¹/₂	cup
some	kirsch (cherry brandy)		some

Dough:

GREASE and flour a 25 cm (10") tube pan.

SIFT flour into a mixing bowl. Add yeast. Mix well.

MAKE a well in the centre. Put salt, egg yolks, sugar, vanilla sugar, flavouring concentrate, butter and milk in the well.

KNEAD dough with an electric mixer fitted with dough hooks on high speed until dough is smooth, blistery and no longer sticky.

COVER. Let rest in a warm place for 40 minutes.

KNEAD dough again.

PLACE dough in prepared pan. Let rest in a warm place for 20 minutes.

PREHEAT oven to 190°C (375°F).

BAKE for 25-30 minutes.

Topping:

PLACE apricot halves in a bowl.

SPRINKLE with kirsch and icing sugar.

CHILL for 1 hour.

Cherry Cream Sauce:

IN a double boiler, combine egg yolks, icing sugar and orange peel. (Temperature of water should be 80°C /150°F.)

BEAT until thick and fluffy.

REMOVE from heat. Continue beating until mixture has cooled.

IN a mixing bowl, beat whipping cream to stiff peaks.

FOLD into egg yolk mixture gently but thoroughly.

ADD kirsch, to taste.

TOP bread ring with apricot halves.

SERVE with cherry cream sauce.

75

Strawberry Tarts

Erdbeertorteletts

Recipe No. 716

Batter:
Marzipan Layer Cake
(See Recipe No. 691)

Cream Filling:

4	egg yolks	4
80 g	icing sugar, sifted	³/₄ cup
1 pkg	**oetker** vanilla sugar (9 g)	1 pkg
250 mL	milk	1 cup
6 sheets	**oetker** gelatin sheets	6 sheets
250 mL	whipping cream	1 cup
60 mL	Grand Marnier	4 tbsp
10-12	strawberries	10-12

Brushing:

some	apricot jam, heated	some

Decoration:

250 mL	whipping cream	1 cup
some	strawberries	some

Batter:

PREPARE marzipan layer cake as directed on page 27.

LINE muffin tins with slices of baked layer cake, 3 mm (¹/₈") thick.

Cream Filling:

IN a mixing bowl, beat egg yolks, icing sugar and vanilla sugar until thick and fluffy.

IN a saucepan, bring milk to a boil.

STIRRING constantly, add egg yolk mixture to the milk. Return to a boil.

PREPARE gelatin according to package directions. STIR into hot egg yolk mixture. Chill.

IN another mixing bowl, beat whipping cream to stiff peaks.

ADD Grand Marnier, to taste.

WHEN egg yolk mixture begins to set, fold in whipped cream gently but thoroughly.

FILL prepared pans halfway with cream. Top with a strawberry.

FILL to the top with cream. Chill for 2-3 hours.

DIP pans quickly in hot water. Turn onto baking sheet. Transfer to dessert plates.

BRUSH with apricot jam.

Decoration:

BEAT whipping cream to stiff peaks.

DECORATE tarts with strawberries and whipped cream.

Fruit Baskets

Bouchet "Singapur"

Recipe No. 717

Meringue:

3	egg whites	3
1 mL	cream of tartar	1/4 tsp
110 g	sugar	1/2 cup
1 pkg	**oetker** vanilla sugar (9 g)	1 pkg

Fruit Cocktail:

1/2	honeydew melon	1/2
1	pear	1
2	peaches	2
3	kiwi fruits	3
some	tangerine slices	some
some	strawberries	some
some	icing sugar, sifted	some
some	coconut liqueur	some

Decoration:

250 mL	whipping cream	1 cup
1 pkg	**oetker** Whip it (10 g)	1 pkg

Meringue:

PREHEAT oven to 120°C (250°F). Line a baking sheet with parchment paper.
BEAT egg whites until frothy.
SIFT cream of tartar over surface, continue beating.
GRADUALLY beat in sugar and vanilla sugar.
CONTINUE beating until sugar has dissolved and mixture is stiff.
PLACE mixture in a pastry bag fitted with a medium plain tube.
PIPE baskets onto prepared baking sheet.
BAKE for 60 minutes. Turn oven off, leaving meringues in oven.

Fruit Cocktail:

PEEL and cube fruit. Place in a bowl.
ADD icing sugar and liqueur. Gently toss.
FILL baskets with fruit mixture.

Decoration:

IN a mixing bowl, beat whipping cream and Whip it to stiff peaks.
PLACE whipped cream in a pastry bag fitted with a star tube.
DECORATE baskets.

Quark Doughnuts with Apricot Sauce

Topfenmäuse

Recipe No. 718

Dough:

410 g	all-purpose flour	2³/₄ cups
1 pkg	**oetker** instant dry yeast (7 g)	1 pkg
30 mL	butter, melted	2 tbsp
30 mL	sugar	2 tbsp
2	egg yolks	2
2	eggs	2
30 mL	whipping cream	2 tbsp
pinch	salt	pinch
300 g	quark, strained	1¹/₃ cups

Deep Frying:

some	vegetable oil	some

Dusting:

1 pkg	**oetker** vanilla sugar (9 g)	1 pkg
45 mL	icing sugar, sifted	3 tbsp

Apricot Sauce:

375 mL	apricot jam	1¹/₂ cups
50 mL	water	¹/₄ cup
	juice of 1 lemon	
some	rum	some

Dough:

SIFT flour into a mixing bowl.
ADD yeast. Mix well.
MAKE a well in the centre. Put butter, sugar, egg yolks, eggs, whipping cream, salt and quark in the well.
KNEAD dough with an electric mixer fitted with dough hooks on high speed until dough is smooth, blistery and no longer sticky.
COVER. Let rest in a warm place until doubled in size.
KNEAD dough again. Cut off pieces 2-3 cm (1-1¹/₄") in length. Shape into balls.
LET rest in a warm place for 15 minutes.
FILL a deep fryer half way with vegetable oil.
HEAT slowly. During the frying process the temperature should be kept at a constant, 180°C (350°F).
PLACE dough in hot oil. Deep fry until golden brown.
REMOVE from oil with slotted spoon and drain on paper towels. Place on wire cooling rack.

Dusting:

MIX together vanilla sugar and icing sugar.
DUST doughnuts with sugar mixture.

Apricot Sauce:

IN a saucepan, combine apricot jam, water, lemon juice and rum. Bring to a boil.
SERVE with doughnuts.

*B*abas with Red Wine Sauce

Rotwein-Baba mit Baisermantel

Recipe No. 719

Dough:

350 g	all-purpose flour	2²/₃ cups	
1 pkg	**oetker** instant dry yeast (7 g)	1 pkg	
pinch	salt	pinch	
50 g	sugar	¹/₄ cup	
1 pkg	**oetker** vanilla sugar (9 g)	1 pkg	
¹/₂ btl	**oetker** lemon flavour-ing concentrate (1 mL)	¹/₂ btl	
2	egg yolks	2	
2	eggs	2	
175 mL	butter, melted	³/₄ cup	
125 mL	milk, lukewarm	¹/₂ cup	

Meringue:

2	egg whites	2	
30 mL	sugar	2 tbsp	

Red Wine Sauce:

250 mL	red wine	1 cup	
70 g	sugar	¹/₃ cup	
15 mL	honey	1 tbsp	
1	clove	1	
1 mL	cinnamon	¹/₄ tsp	
5 drops	**oetker** lemon flavour-ing concentrate	5 drops	
80 g	raisins	¹/₂ cup	

Dough:

BRUSH several oven safe dariole molds with butter.

SIFT flour into a mixing bowl. Add yeast. Mix well.

MAKE a well in the centre. Put salt, sugar, vanilla sugar, flavouring concentrate, egg yolks, eggs, butter and milk in the well.

KNEAD dough with an electric mixer fitted with dough hooks on high speed until dough is smooth, blistery and no longer sticky.

COVER. Let rest in a warm place until dough has doubled in size.

FILL molds halfway with dough. Place on a baking sheet.

COVER. Let rest until doubled in size.

PREHEAT oven to 200°C (400°F).

BAKE for 12-15 minutes.

AFTER baking, remove babas from molds immediately. Place 8 cm (3") apart on a baking sheet.

Meringue:

BEAT egg whites and sugar to stiff peaks.

PLACE beaten egg white in a pastry bag fitted with a star tube. Decorate babas.

RETURN to oven.

BAKE for 5 minutes.

Red Wine Sauce:

IN a saucepan, combine wine, sugar, honey, spices, flavouring concentrate and raisins.

BRING to a boil.

SERVE warm sauce with babas.

Cold Desserts

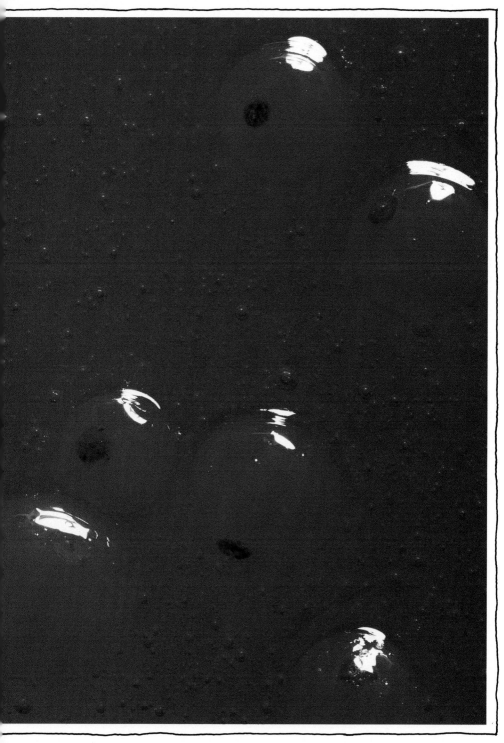

Apples in Cranberry Sauce

Apfeligel auf Preiselbeeren

Recipe No. 720

Ingredients:

10	small apples	10
500 mL	white wine	2 cups
250 g	sugar	1 cup
	juice of 2 lemons	
1	cinnamon stick	1
2	cloves	2

Filling:

1 pkg	**oetker** chocolate mousse (87 g)	1 pkg
250 mL	milk	1 cup

Decoration:

150 g	almonds, slivered, toasted	1 cup

Cranberry Sauce:

5 mL	**oetker** Gustin corn starch	1 tsp
	some wine	some
1 can	cranberry sauce (398 mL/14 fl oz)	1 can

PEEL and core apples.
IN a large saucepan, combine wine, sugar, lemon juice, cinnamon stick and cloves.
BRING to a boil.
ADD apples. Cook until liquid evaporates.
REMOVE apples from saucepan. Cool completely.

Filling:
PREPARE chocolate mousse according to package directions.
SPOON or pipe mousse into cored apples.
IF desired, insert almond slivers into the outside of the apples.

Cranberry Sauce:
IN a saucepan, combine corn starch and wine.
ADD cranberry sauce and bring to a boil.
REDUCE heat and simmer for 5 minutes. Cool completely.
SPOON sauce onto dessert plates. Place apples in the centre of the sauce.

*B*lanched Pears

*B*lanchierte Birnen

Recipe No. 721

Ingredients:

3	pears	3	
15 mL	lemon juice	1 tbsp	
125 mL	white wine	1/2 cup	
45 mL	honey	3 tbsp	
1 mL	cinnamon	1/4 tsp	

Pear Sauce:

250 mL	whipping cream	1 cup	
5 mL	honey	1 tsp	
50 g	almonds, ground	1/2 cup	
some	pear liqueur	some	

Decoration:

some	cranberry sauce	some	

PEEL and slice pears lengthwise. Core.
SPRINKLE with lemon juice.
IN a saucepan, combine wine, honey and cinnamon. Bring to a boil.
PLACE pear halves in the wine mixture, two at a time. Blanch for 3 minutes. Using a slotted spoon, remove pears from saucepan.
COOL completely.

Pear Sauce:

IN a mixing bowl, beat whipping cream and honey to semi-stiff peaks.
FOLD in almonds gently but thoroughly.
ADD pear liqueur, to taste.
SPOON sauce onto dessert plates.
PLACE pears in centre of pear sauce.
DECORATE with cranberry sauce.

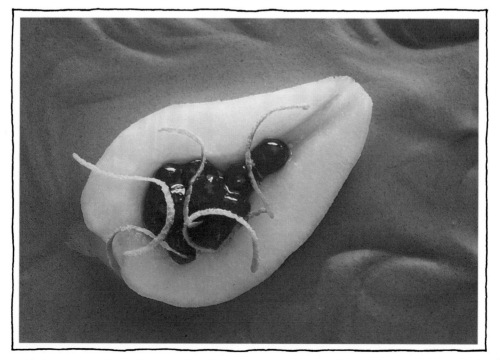

Tuile Delights

Honigtopfen im Stanitzel

Recipe No. 722

Tuile Mixture:

4	egg whites	4
100 g	sugar	$^1/_2$ cup
50 mL	butter, melted and cooled	$^1/_4$ cup
pinch	salt	pinch
1 mL	cinnamon	$^1/_4$ tsp
100 g	all-purpose flour	$^3/_4$ cup
$^1/_2$ btl	**oetker** almond flavouring concentrate (1 mL)	$^1/_2$ btl

Quark Filling:

500 g	quark	2 cups
125 mL	honey	$^1/_2$ cup
$^1/_2$ btl	**oetker** lemon flavouring concentrate (1 mL)	$^1/_2$ btl
60 mL	plum brandy	4 tbsp
6 sheets	**oetker** gelatin sheets	6 sheets

Raspberry Puree:

150 g	raspberries	$1^1/_4$ cups
30 g	icing sugar, sifted	$^1/_4$ cup
500 mL	yogurt	2 cups

Decoration:

500 g	apricot halves	3 cups
3	nectarines	3

Tuile Mixture:

PREHEAT oven to 190°C (375°F). Grease a baking sheet.

IN a mixing bowl, beat egg whites and sugar until frothy.

GENTLY but thoroughly fold in butter, salt, cinnamon, flour and flavouring concentrate.

STIR until mixture is smooth.

DROP mixture by the tablespoon, 8 cm (3") apart, onto prepared baking sheet.

FLATTEN mixture, using a fork dipped in ice water, to a diameter of 10 cm (4").

BAKE 5-6 minutes or until outside of each tuile is golden brown.

IMMEDIATELY remove baked tuiles with a lifter. (Clean lifter after removing a tuile from the baking sheet.)

WHILE warm, roll tuiles to form cones. (Remove only as many slices as can be rolled.)

REPEAT process until mixture is used up.

Quark Filling:

IN a mixing bowl, combine quark, honey, flavouring concentrate and plum brandy.

MIX well.

PREPARE gelatin according to package directions. Fold into quark mixture. Chill.

WHEN quark mixture begins to set, place mixture in a pastry bag fitted with a star tube.

PIPE mixture into cones.

Raspberry Puree:

IN a blender, combine raspberries and icing sugar. Puree.

BLEND in yogurt.

SERVE cones with apricot halves, nectarines and raspberry puree.

Chocolate Pyramids with Fruit

Schokopyramide mit Früchten

Recipe No. 723

Ingredients:

250	mL	milk	1 cup
1	pkg	**oetker** vanilla sugar (9 g)	1 pkg
5	drops	**oetker** lemon flavouring concentrate	5 drops
	pinch	salt	pinch
50	g	cream of wheat	4 tbsp
6	sheets	**oetker** gelatin sheets	6 sheets
2		egg yolks	2
80	g	icing sugar, sifted	²/₃ cup
125	mL	whipped cream	¹/₂ cup
15	mL	Grand Marnier	1 tbsp
60	g	chocolate, melted	4 squares

Decoration:

	some	raspberries	some
	some	peach slices	some

IN a saucepan, bring milk, vanilla sugar, flavouring concentrate and salt to a boil. STIRRING constantly, add cream of wheat. COOK for 5 minutes.

REMOVE from heat. Cover. Let stand for 15 minutes.

PREPARE gelatin according to package directions.

IN a mixing bowl, beat egg yolks and icing sugar until fluffy.

FOLD egg mixture and gelatin into the hot cream of wheat mixture.

WHEN mixture begins to set, stir in whipped cream and Grand Marnier.

STIR chocolate into one-third of the mixture.

SPREAD remaining two-thirds of white mixture 2 cm (1") thick on the bottom and up the sides of a 10 cm (4") dish or container.

RESERVE some white mixture to cover the chocolate mixture.

TURN chocolate mixture into the dish.

COVER with reserved white mixture. Chill for 2-3 hours.

DIP pan quickly in hot water. Turn onto a serving platter.

SLICE on the diagonal. Cut into pyramid shapes.

SERVE with raspberries and peach slices.

Raspberry Sorbet

Himbeersorbet

Recipe No. 724

Ingredients:

250 g	raspberries	2	cups
125 mL	water	$^1/_2$	cup
125 mL	white wine	$^1/_2$	cup
	juice of 1 lemon		
15 mL	honey	1	tbsp
80 g	sugar	$^1/_3$	cup

Liquid:

champagne, wine or fruit juice

IN a blender, combine raspberries, water, wine, lemon juice, honey and sugar.
PUREE mixture.
PLACE in freezer for 3-4 hours, stirring occasionally.
BEAT frozen mixture with a hand mixer. Spoon into dessert bowls.
ADD liquid, as desired and serve.

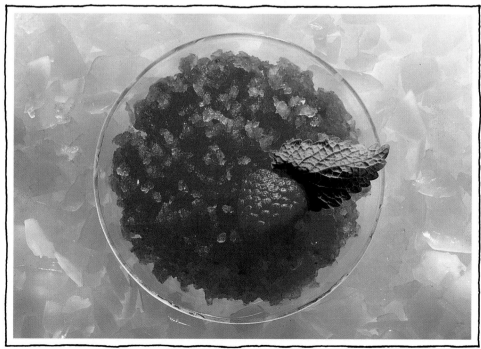

*P*ear Triangles

*B*irnendreispitz

Recipe No. 725

Batter:
Marzipan Layer Cake
(See Recipe No. 691)

Filling:

250	mL	milk	1 cup
80	g	sugar	⅓ cup
2		egg yolks	2
1	pkg	**oetker** vanilla sugar (9 g)	1 pkg
80	g	chocolate, softened	5 squares
6	sheets	**oetker** gelatin sheets	6 sheets
1	can	pears, cubed (398 mL/14 fl oz)	1 can
250	mL	whipping cream	1 cup
30-45	mL	pear schnaps	2-3 tbsp

Batter:
PREPARE marzipan layer cake as directed on page 27.
*LINE a terrine dish or a 23 x 12 cm (9 x 5")
loaf pan with baked slices of layer cake, 3 mm
(⅛") thick.*

Filling:
*IN a saucepan, combine milk, sugar, egg yolks,
vanilla sugar and chocolate.*
*HEAT to a temperature of 80°C (150°F), while
stirring constantly.*
*PREPARE gelatin according to package
directions.*
ADD to hot milk mixture.
*DRAIN pears. Fold into milk mixture gently
but thoroughly. Chill.*
*IN a mixing bowl, beat whipping cream to stiff
peaks.*
*WHEN milk mixture begins to set, add whipped
cream and pear schnaps.*
SPOON mixture into prepared pan.
CHILL for 2-3 hours or until set.
*DIP pan quickly in hot water. Turn onto a
serving platter.*
*CUT pastry into 1 cm (⅜") slices. Halve these
on the diagonal.*

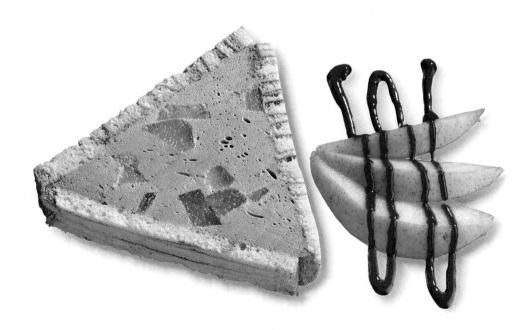

Rice Pudding with Mango Sauce

Reistörtchen mit Mangopüree

Recipe No. 726

Ingredients:

375 mL	milk	1¹/₂ cups	
pinch	salt	pinch	
45 mL	sugar	3 tbsp	
60 g	rice	¹/₄ cup	
3 sheets	**oetker** gelatin sheets	3 sheets	
125 mL	whipping cream	¹/₂ cup	
5 drops	**oetker** lemon flavouring concentrate	5 drops	
5 drops	**oetker** rum flavouring concentrate	5 drops	

Mango Puree:

2	ripe mangoes	2	
15 mL	icing sugar, sifted	1 tbsp	

Decoration:

250 g	strawberries	2 cups	
some	icing sugar, sifted	some	

IN a saucepan, bring milk, salt, and sugar to a boil.

SPRINKLE rice into milk mixture. Continue cooking until rice is done.

PREPARE gelatin according to package directions.

ADD to the warm rice. Cool completely.

IN a mixing bowl, beat whipping cream to stiff peaks.

FOLD whipped cream and flavouring concentrates into the rice mixture gently but thoroughly.

FILL muffin tins with rice mixture. Chill for 2-3 hours.

Mango Puree:

PEEL, pit and chop mangoes.

IN a blender, purée mango and sugar.

DIP muffin tins quickly in hot water. Turn onto baking sheet. Transfer to dessert plates.

SERVE with mango puree and strawberries.

DUST lightly with icing sugar.

Pineapple Quark on Marzipan Petals

Früchtetopfen auf Hippenblatt
Recipe No. 727

Marzipan mixture:

100 g	icing sugar, sifted	1	cup
30 g	marzipan	1	oz
2	small eggs	2	
90 g	all-purpose flour	²/₃	cup
pinch	salt		pinch
1 mL	cinnamon	¹/₄	tsp
2 mL	cocoa	¹/₂	tsp

Fruit Quark:

500 g	quark	2	cups
50 mL	honey	¹/₄	cup
2 pkgs	**oetker** vanilla sugar (18 g)	2	pkgs
1 can	pineapple, crushed (540 mL/19 fl oz)	1	can
6 sheets	**oetker** gelatin sheets	6	sheets

Strawberry Sauce:

250 g	strawberries	2	cups
80 g	icing sugar, sifted	²/₃	cup
some	brandy		some
some	pineapple pieces		some

Marzipan Mixture:
PREHEAT oven to 180°C (350°F).
IN a mixing bowl, combine icing sugar, marzipan and one egg. Stir until mixture is smooth.
STIR in remaining egg. (The mixture should not be fluffy.)
ADD flour, salt and cinnamon. Stir well.
COVER and chill for 2 hours.
ADD cocoa to 15 mL (1 tbsp) of the mixture.
PLACE cocoa mixture in a small pastry bag fitted with a fine tube.
LINE a baking sheet with parchment paper.
DRAW 6 petal shapes 10 cm (4") in diameter on the parchment paper.
GENTLY spread batter to fill petal shapes.
PIPE desired patterns on marzipan mixture with chocolate mixture.
BAKE for 10 minutes.
IMMEDIATELY after baking, remove petals using a lifter. (Remove only as many petals as can be shaped.)
PLACE a drinking glass in the centre of each warm petal. Pull individual petals upwards.
COOL completely. Remove glass.
REPEAT process until all the marzipan mixture has been used up.

Fruit Quark:
IN a mixing bowl, combine quark, honey, vanilla sugar and crushed pineapple.
PREPARE gelatin according to package directions.
ADD to quark mixture. Chill.
WHEN quark mixture begins to set, place mixture in a pastry bag fitted with a star tube.
PIPE cream into the centre of each marzipan petal.

Strawberry Sauce:
IN a blender, combine strawberries and icing sugar. Puree.
ADD brandy, to taste.
SERVE sauce with marzipan petals.
DECORATE with pineapple pieces.

93

*I*ced Bundt with Poppy Seeds

*E*isguglhupf mit Mohn

Recipe No. 728

Ingredients:

120 g	poppy seeds, ground	1	cup
125 mL	milk	¹/₂	cup
125 g	sugar	¹/₂	cup
4	egg yolks	4	
15 mL	honey	1	tbsp
1 pkg	**oetker** vanilla sugar (9 g)	1	pkg
500 mL	whipping cream	2	cups

Decoration:

1 can	cranberry sauce (398 mL/14 fl oz)	1	can
some	apricot halves, canned		some

IN a saucepan, bring poppy seeds, milk and sugar to a boil. Remove from heat and chill.

IN a mixing bowl, beat egg yolks, honey and vanilla sugar until fluffy.

IN another bowl, beat whipping cream to stiff peaks.

FOLD whipped cream and poppy seed mixture into the egg yolk mixture gently but thoroughly.

RINSE several mini Bundt pans with cold water.

SPOON mixture into pans.

CHILL in the freezer for 2-4 hours.

DIP pans quickly in hot water. Turn onto dessert plates.

Decoration:

ADD some apricot juice to the cranberry sauce to dilute.

SERVE dessert with cranberry mixture and apricot halves.

Glazed Berries with Rum Sauce

Waldbeerensülze mit Rumsoße

Recipe No. 729

Ingredients:

250 g	raspberries	2 cups	
250 g	blueberries	1³/₄ cups	
100 g	icing sugar, sifted	1 cup	
some	rum	some	
2 pkgs	**oetker** instant clear glaze (60 g)	2 pkgs	
250 mL	white wine	1 cup	
250 mL	water or fruit juice	1 cup	

Rum Sauce:

¹/₂ pkg	**oetker** vanilla pudding (21 g)	¹/₂ pkg	
500 mL	milk	2 cups	
45 mL	sugar	3 tbsp	
30 mL	rum	2 tbsp	

IN a mixing bowl, gently toss raspberries, blueberries, icing sugar and rum. Chill for 1 hour.

PREPARE glaze with white wine and water or fruit juice, according to package directions.

RINSE several mini bundt molds with cold water.

LINE bottom of molds with berry mixture.

FILL with glaze. Chill until set.

Rum Sauce:

IN a mixing bowl, add 125 mL (¹/₂ cup) of the measured milk to the pudding.

IN a saucepan, bring remaining milk and sugar to a boil.

ADD pudding mixture to the milk mixture.

RETURN to a boil, while stirring. Remove from heat and let cool. Stir several times to prevent skin from forming on the surface.

ADD rum.

DIP molds quickly in hot water. Turn onto dessert plates.

SERVE with rum sauce.

95

Fruity Towers

Fruchttürmchen

Recipe No. 730

Strawberry Cream:

250 mL	milk	1	cup
80 g	sugar	1/3	cup
1 pkg	**oetker** vanilla sugar (9 g)	1	pkg
5 drops	**oetker** lemon flavour-ing concentrate	5	drops
6 sheets	**oetker** gelatin sheets	6	sheets
125 mL	strawberries, pureed	1/2	cup
250 g	quark or cream cheese	1	cup
125 mL	whipping cream	1/2	cup
some	strawberries		some

Apricot Cream:

250 mL	milk	1	cup
80 g	sugar	1/3	cup
1 pkg	**oetker** vanilla sugar (9 g)	1	pkg
5 drops	**oetker** lemon flavour-ing concentrate	5	drops
6 sheets	**oetker** gelatin sheets	6	sheets
125 mL	apricots, pureed	1/2	cup
250 g	quark or cream cheese	1	cup
125 mL	whipping cream	1/2	cup

Strawberry Sauce:

250 g	strawberries	2	cups
50 g	sugar	1/4	cup
some	brandy		some

Decoration:

some	sour cream		some

Strawberry Cream:

IN a saucepan, combine milk, sugar, vanilla sugar, and flavouring concentrate.

PREPARE gelatin according to package directions. Add to saucepan.

HEAT mixture to a temperature of 80°C (150°F), while stirring constantly. Let cool.

WHEN mixture begins to set, add pureed strawberries and quark (or beaten cream cheese).

IN a mixing bowl, beat whipping cream to stiff peaks. Fold into strawberry mixture gently but thoroughly.

RINSE several, small soufflé pans with water.

LINE the bottom of the pans with strawberries.

FILL halfway with strawberry cream.

Apricot Cream:

FOLLOW method for strawberry cream.

ADD to strawberry cream in pans. Fill to the top.

Strawberry Sauce:

IN a blender, puree strawberries, sugar and brandy.

DIP pans quickly in hot water. Turn onto dessert plates.

SERVE with strawberry sauce and sour cream.

*F*ruit Ring

*F*ruchtring

Recipe No. 731

Cherry Jelly:

1	pkg	**oetker** instant clear glaze (30 g)	1 pkg
250	mL	cherry juice	1 cup
250	g	sour cherries, pitted	1½ cups

Orange Jelly:

1	pkg	**oetker** instant clear glaze (30 g)	1 pkg
250	mL	orange juice	1 cup
1	can	mandarin oranges (284 mL/10 fl oz)	1 can

Pear Jelly:

1	pkg	**oetker** instant clear glaze (30 g)	1 pkg
250	mL	pear juice	1 cup
1	can	pears, cubed (398 mL/14 fl oz)	1 can

Vanilla Sauce:

1	pkg	**oetker** instant vanilla sauce (35 g)	1 pkg
250	mL	milk	1 cup

Cherry Jelly:

RINSE a 22 cm (9") in diameter ringform pan with cold water.
PREPARE glaze according to package directions, using cherry juice.
POUR one-half of the glaze into the form.
WHEN mixture begins to set, top with cherries.
TOP with remaining glaze. (If remaining half of glaze sets, heat to soften.)
CHILL until set.

Orange Jelly and Pear Jelly:

REPEAT process with orange and pear jelly.
CHILL entire mixture for 3 hours.
DIP form quickly in hot water. Turn onto a serving platter.

Vanilla Sauce:

PREPARE vanilla sauce according to package directions.
SERVE with slices of fruit ring.

Cream Delights with Black Currant Sauce

Grießflammerie

Recipe No. 732

Ingredients:

500	mL	milk	2 cups
1	pkg	**oetker** vanilla sugar (9 g)	1 pkg
1	btl	**oetker** lemon flavouring concentrate (2 mL)	1 btl
	pinch	salt	pinch
70	g	cream of wheat	¹/₃ cup
8	sheets	**oetker** gelatin sheets	8 sheets
4		egg yolks	4
50	g	sugar (first amount)	¹/₄ cup
4		egg whites	4
50	g	sugar (second amount)	¹/₄ cup
250	mL	whipping cream	1 cup
800	g	grapes, peeled, seeded	5 cups

Black Currant Sauce:

600	g	black currants	1¹/₂ cups
125	mL	white wine, heated	¹/₂ cup
100	g	icing sugar, sifted	³/₄ cup
		juice of 1 lemon	
30	mL	cassis liqueur	2 tbsp
	some	sour cream	some

IN a saucepan, bring milk, vanilla sugar, flavouring concentrate and salt to a boil. SLOWLY stir in cream of wheat. Heat until mixture is creamy.

PREPARE gelatin according to package directions. ADD to cream of wheat mixture.

IN a mixing bowl, beat egg yolks and sugar until fluffy.

FOLD into cream of wheat mixture gently but thoroughly.

IN another bowl, beat egg whites and sugar to stiff peaks.

FOLD into cream of wheat mixture gently but thoroughly.

BEAT whipping cream to stiff peaks. Fold into cream of wheat mixture.

SPOON mixture into chilled savarin molds. TOP with a few grapes. Chill for 2-3 hours.

Black Currant Sauce:

IN a bowl, marinate black currants in wine for 50-60 minutes.

ADD icing sugar, lemon juice and cassis liqueur. Transfer to a blender. Puree.

DIP molds quickly in hot water. Turn onto dessert plates. Top with grapes.

SERVE with Cassis sauce. Dab with sour cream.

99

Avocados with Fruit and Lemon Sorbet

Avocados mit Früchten und Zitroneneis

Recipe No. 733

Ingredients:

2	avocados	2
30 mL	icing sugar, sifted	2 tbsp
30 mL	brandy	2 tbsp

Decoration:

some	lemon sorbet	some
1 can	mandarins (284 mL/10 fl oz)	1 can
1 can	cherries, sour, pitted (398 mL/14 fl oz)	1 can
some	strawberries	some
some	walnut halves	some

CUT avocados lengthwise. Separate carefully.
REMOVE pits.
USING a spoon, scrape out the fruit flesh.
STRAIN through a sieve.
ADD icing sugar and brandy.
SPOON fruit mixture into the hollow skins.
DECORATE with lemon sorbet, fruits and nuts.

Pear Timbales

Birnentimbal

Recipe No. 734

Ingredients:

500 mL	milk	2 cups	
pinch	salt	pinch	
1 pkg	**oetker** vanilla sugar (9 g)	1 pkg	
½ btl	**oetker** lemon flavour-ing concentrate (1 mL)	½ btl	
70 g	cream of wheat	⅓ cup	
4	egg yolks	4	
150 g	icing sugar, sifted	1⅓ cups	
12 sheets	**oetker** gelatin sheets	12 sheets	
250 mL	whipping cream	1 cup	
30 mL	pear liqueur	2 tbsp	

Chocolate Topping:

1 pkg	**oetker** Chocofix (100 g)	1 pkg	

Decoration:

1 can	pears, cubed (540 mL/19 fl oz)	1 can	
some	pistachio nuts	some	

IN a saucepan, bring milk, salt, vanilla sugar and flavouring concentrate to a boil.

SLOWLY stir in cream of wheat. Cook for 5 minutes. Cover and let rest.

IN a mixing bowl, beat egg yolks and icing sugar until fluffy.

FOLD egg yolk mixture into the hot cream of wheat mixture gently but thoroughly.

PREPARE gelatin according to package directions.

STIR into cream of wheat mixture. Cool completely.

IN another bowl, beat whipping cream to stiff peaks.

WHEN the cream of wheat mixture begins to set, fold in whipped cream and pear liqueur.

RINSE muffin tins with cold water.

FILL muffin tins with mixture. Chill for 2 hours. Loosen edges with a knife. Dip tins quickly in hot water. Turn onto baking sheet.

TRANSFER to serving plates.

Chocolate Topping:

PREPARE Chocofix according to package directions.

SERVE Chocofix, cubed pears and pistachio nuts with pear timbales.

Marzipan Rolls with Kiwi Sauce

Marsalarolle mit Kiwisoße

Recipe No. 735

Marzipan Mixture:

200 g	icing sugar, sifted	2	cups
60 g	marzipan	2	oz
1 mL	cinnamon	1/4	tsp
pinch	salt		pinch
3	eggs	3	
170 g	all-purpose flour	1 1/3	cups
5 mL	cocoa	1	tsp

Wine Cream:

375 mL	Marsala wine	1 1/2	cups
6	egg yolks	6	
120 g	icing sugar, sifted	1	cup
7 sheets	**oetker** gelatin sheets	7	sheets
	juice of 1 lemon		
1 mL	cinnamon	1/4	tsp
60 mL	brandy	4	tbsp
375 mL	whipping cream	1 1/2	cups

Kiwi Sauce:

6	kiwi fruit	6	

Decoration:

some	mandarin slices		some

Marzipan Mixture:
PREHEAT oven to 180°C (350°F). Grease a baking sheet.
IN a mixing bowl, combine icing sugar, marzipan, cinnamon, salt and one egg. Stir until mixture is smooth.
QUICKLY add remaining eggs (the mixture should not become fluffy).
BLEND in flour.
COVER. Chill for 2-3 hours.

ADD cocoa to 30 mL (2 tbsp) of the mixture.
PLACE mixture in a small pastry bag fitted with a small, plain tube.
DROP batter by the tablespoon onto prepared baking sheet.
USING a fork dipped in ice water, shape batter into 10 cm (4") squares.
PIPE cocoa mixture on the squares.
BAKE for 10 minutes.
IMMEDIATELY after baking, remove marzipan squares from baking sheet using a lifter.
BEND warm marzipan squares around the handle of a wooden spoon. (Remove only as many squares as can be shaped.)
CONTINUE until all of the mixture is used up.

Wine Cream:
IN a saucepan, bring wine to a boil.
IN a mixing bowl, beat egg yolks and icing sugar until fluffy.
STIR wine into egg yolk mixture.
PREPARE gelatin according to package directions.
STIR gelatin, lemon juice, cinnamon and brandy into the wine mixture.
COOL completely.
IN another mixing bowl, beat whipping cream to stiff peaks.
WHEN the wine mixture begins to set, fold in whipped cream.
PLACE mixture in a pastry bag fitted with a round plain tube.
PIPE mixture down the centre of the rolls.

Kiwi Sauce:
PEEL kiwi.
MASH kiwi with potato masher.
SERVE with marzipan rolls.
DECORATE with sliced mandarin oranges.

103

Creamy Clouds

Meraner Creme

Recipe No. 736

Ingredients:

3		egg yolks	3
80	g	icing sugar, sifted (first amount)	³/₄ cup
1	pkg	**oetker** vanilla sugar (9 g)	1 pkg
15	mL	rum	1 tbsp
125	mL	whipping cream	¹/₂ cup
30	mL	icing sugar, sifted (second amount)	2 tbsp

Dipping:

1	pkg	**oetker** Chocofix (100 g)	1 pkg

Decoration:

10-12	ladyfingers	10-12
10-12	grapes	10-12
some	red currant jam	some

IN a mixing bowl, beat egg yolks, icing sugar (first amount), vanilla sugar and rum until fluffy.

IN another bowl, beat whipping cream and icing sugar (second amount) to stiff peaks.

FOLD into egg yolk mixture gently but thoroughly.

SPOON mixture into dessert dishes. Chill for 2 hours.

PREPARE Chocofix according to package directions.

DIP lady fingers in Chocofix.

SERVE dessert with lady fingers, grapes and jam.

104

Riesling Jelly

Rieslinggelee

Recipe No. 737

Ingredients:

375	mL	riesling wine, white	1½	cups
6	sheets	**oetker** gelatin sheets	6	sheets
2	pkgs	**oetker** vanilla sugar (18 g)	2	pkgs
250	g	white and blue grapes	1½	cups

Vanilla Sauce:

1	pkg	**oetker** instant vanilla sauce (35 g)	1	pkg
250	mL	milk	1	cup
	some	brandy		some

Decoration:

some	**oetker** Chocofix (100 g)	some
some	white and blue grapes	some

IN a saucepan, heat wine to a temperature of 70°C (150°F).
PREPARE gelatin according to package directions.
SLOWLY stir gelatin and vanilla sugar into wine.
RINSE small ring molds with cold water.
PLACE grapes in bottom of molds.
WHEN wine mixture begins to set, spoon over grapes.
CHILL for 3-4 hours.

Sauce:
PREPARE instant vanilla sauce according to package directions. Let cool slightly.
ADD brandy, to taste.

PREPARE Chocofix according to package directions.
PLACE a small amount of Chocofix into a pastry bag fitted with a fine tube.
PIPE grape vines onto a piece of parchment paper. Let set. Remove.
DIP molds quickly in hot water. Turn onto dessert plates.
SERVE with vanilla sauce, chocolate vines and grapes.

105

*A*pples with Praline Sauce

Weinapfel auf Nougatmousselin

Recipe No. 738

Ingredients:

3	apples	3
500 mL	white wine	2 cups
60 g	sugar	1/4 cup
1 pkg	**oetker** vanilla sugar (9 g)	1 pkg
	juice of 1 lemon	
30	lady fingers	30

Chocolate Mousse:

1 pkg	**oetker** chocolate mousse (87 g)	1 pkg
250 mL	milk	1 cup

Praline Sauce:

250 mL	milk	1 cup
250 mL	whipping cream	1 cup
100 g	nougat	3.5 oz
1 pkg	**oetker** vanilla sugar (9 g)	1 pkg
2	egg yolks	2
15 mL	**oetker** vanilla pudding	1 tbsp
30 mL	kirsch (cherry brandy)	2 tbsp

Decoration:

some	chocolate, shaved	some
some	red jam	some

PEEL and core apples. Cut into 2 cm (1")
slices.
IN a saucepan, bring wine, sugar, vanilla
sugar and lemon juice to a boil.
ADD apples and cook until semi-soft. Let cool.
PLACE three ladyfingers on a dessert plate.
POSITION apple slices over lady fingers.

Chocolate Mousse:
PREPARE chocolate mousse according to
package directions.
PIPE over apple slices.

Praline Sauce:
IN a saucepan, combine milk, whipping cream,
nougat, vanilla sugar, egg yolks and pudding.
BRING to a boil while stirring constantly. Let
cool. Add kirsch.
POUR sauce around apple slices.
DECORATE with chocolate shavings and dot
with jam.

Tip: The apple slices look particulary
attractive when cut with a cookie cutter.

Warm Desserts

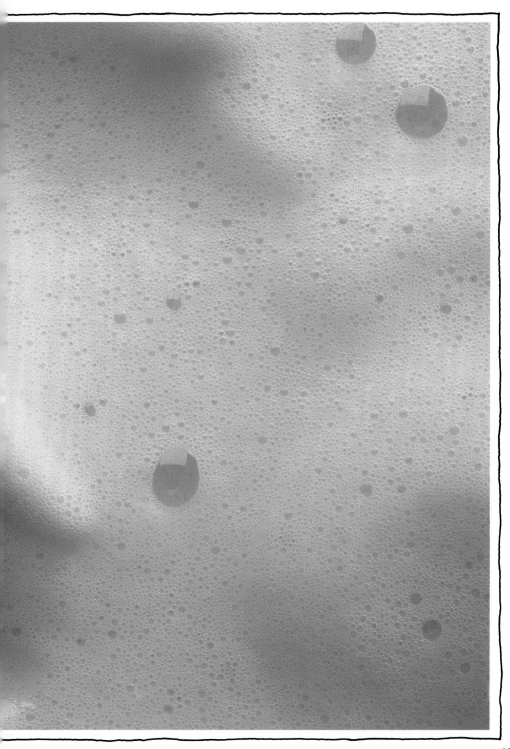

Apple Zabaglione

Apfelweinschaum

Recipe No. 739

Ingredients:

1	lemon	1	
4	apples, sour, red	4	
30 mL	butter	2	tbsp
30 mL	almonds, sliced	2	tbsp
2	egg yolks	2	
1 pkg	**oetker** vanilla sugar (9 g)	1	pkg
15 mL	honey	1	tbsp
pinch	cinnamon		pinch
125 mL	apple cider	1/2	cup

ZEST lemon. Squeeze lemon and reserve juice.
WASH and core apples. Cut into thin slices.
SPRINKLE with lemon juice.
IN a saucepan, heat butter.
ADD almond slices. Brown slightly. Remove almonds.
PLACE apple slices in saucepan.
ALLOW liquid to evaporate slightly.
IN a double boiler, combine egg yolks, vanilla sugar, honey, cinnamon, apple cider and a few drops of the reserved lemon juice. Mix well.
ADD remaining liquid from saucepan. Beat until foamy.
SPOON onto dessert plates.
TOP with apple slices.
DECORATE with almond slices and lemon zest.

Rounds in Yogurt Sauce

Grießblatteln mit Joghurtsoße

Recipe No. 740

Ingredients:

500	mL	milk	2 cups
	pinch	salt	pinch
30	mL	sugar	2 tbsp
200	g	cream of wheat	1 cup
1	pkg	**oetker** vanilla sugar (9 g)	1 pkg
50	g	raisins	1/3 cup

Brushing:

30	mL	butter, melted	2 tbsp

Sauce:

500	mL	yogurt	2 cups
1	pkg	**oetker** vanilla sugar (9 g)	1 pkg
45	mL	sugar	3 tbsp
1	can	cranberry sauce (398 mL/14 fl oz)	1 can
2	drops	**oetker** rum flavouring concentrate	2 drops

IN a saucepan, bring milk, salt and sugar to a boil.

GRADUALLY add cream of wheat. Cook for 10 minutes.

REMOVE from heat. Cover. Let rest for 20 minutes.

ADD vanilla sugar and raisins.

PREHEAT oven to 200°C (400°F).

SPREAD mixture 2 cm (1") thick on a working surface. Cool completely.

USING a round cookie cutter, cut out slices 5 cm (2") in diameter.

PLACE slices on a baking sheet.

BRUSH with butter.

BAKE for 10 minutes.

Sauce:

IN a mixing bowl, combine yogurt, vanilla sugar, sugar, cranberry sauce and flavouring concentrate. Mix well.

SERVE with rounds.

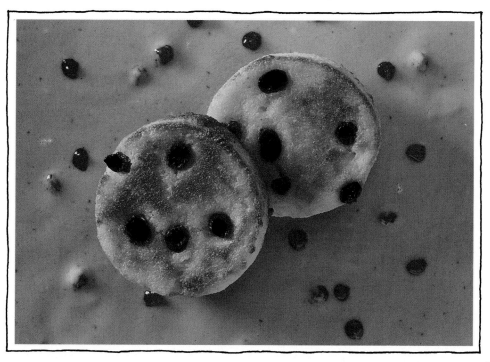

Red Wine Pears with Blueberries

Rotweinbirne mit heidelbeeren

Recipe No. 741

Ingredients:

8	pears	8	
500 mL	red wine	2	cups
1 pkg	**oetker** vanilla sugar (9 g)	1	pkg
200 g	sugar	1	cup
1	cinnamon stick	1	
3	cloves	3	
5 drops	**oetker** lemon flavouring concentrate	5	drops

Blueberry Sauce:

15 mL	**oetker** vanilla pudding	1	tbsp
250 mL	red wine mixture, reserved	1	cup
15 mL	rum	1	tbsp
250 g	blueberries	1³/₄	cups

PEEL pears, leaving the stem attached.
IN a saucepan, bring red wine, vanilla sugar, sugar, cinnamon stick, cloves and flavouring concentrate to a boil.
DISCARD cinnamon stick and cloves.
PLACE pears in a casserole dish. Pour wine mixture over pears.
MARINATE for 20 minutes.
REMOVE pears. Let rest.
ALLOW wine mixture to cool completely.
RESERVE for blueberry sauce.

Blueberry Sauce:

IN a saucepan, bring pudding, 250 mL (1 cup) of the reserved wine mixture and rum to a boil, stirring constantly.
ADD blueberries.
TRANSFER pears to dessert plates.
SERVE with blueberry sauce.

Quark Fritters with Apricot Sauce

Topfenkrapferln mit Marillensoße

Recipe No. 742

Ingredients:

400 g	quark	1½	cups
2	egg yolks	2	
40 g	icing sugar, sifted	⅓	cup
pinch	salt		pinch
½ btl	**oetker** lemon flavour-ing concentrate (1 mL)	½	btl
50 g	raisins	⅓	cup
750 mL	potatoes, cooked, mashed	3	cups
2	egg whites	2	

Brushing:

50 mL	butter, melted	¼	cup

Apricot Sauce:

375 mL	apricot jam	1½	cups
50 mL	water	¼	cup
	juice of 1 lemon		
30 mL	rum	2	tbsp

PREHEAT oven to 200°C (400°F). Grease a baking sheet.

IN a mixing bowl, combine quark, egg yolks, icing sugar, salt, flavouring concentrate and raisins.

FOLD in potatoes gently but thoroughly.

IN another bowl, beat egg whites to stiff peaks.

FOLD into potato-quark mixture.

FLOUR hands. Shape mixture into small patties. Place on prepared baking sheet.

BRUSH with butter.

BAKE for 20 minutes.

Apricot Sauce:

IN a saucepan, bring apricot jam, water, lemon juice and rum to a boil. Mix well.

SERVE sauce with fritters.

Quark and Rice Soufflé with Fruit

Topfenreisauflauf mit Früchten

Recipe No. 743

Ingredients:

750	mL	milk	3 cups
	pinch	salt	pinch
100	g	rice	1 cup
60	g	butter	1/4 cup
50	g	icing sugar, sifted	1/2 cup
4		egg yolks	4
1	btl	**oetker** lemon flavouring concentrate (2 mL)	1 btl
5	drops	**oetker** almond flavouring concentrate	5 drops
45	mL	whipping cream	3 tbsp
250	g	quark	1 cup
2		egg whites	2

Meringue Topping:

2		egg whites	2
30	mL	sugar	2 tbsp

Decoration:

	assorted fruits	

PREHEAT oven to 160°C (325°F). Grease a 20 cm (8") baking pan.

IN a saucepan, bring milk and salt to a boil. STIR in rice. Cook, covered, over low heat for approximately 25 minutes or until done. Let cool.

IN a mixing bowl, beat butter, icing sugar, egg yolks and flavouring concentrates until fluffy. ADD whipping cream and quark. Mix well. FOLD into rice mixture gently but thoroughly. IN another bowl, beat egg whites to stiff peaks. FOLD beaten egg whites into the rice mixture gently but thoroughly.

TURN mixture into prepared pan.

BAKE for 50 minutes.

Meringue Topping:

PREHEAT oven to 200°C (400°F).

BEAT egg whites and sugar to stiff peaks.

PIPE egg white mixture decoratively over the hot rice mixture.

RETURN to oven.

BAKE on upper oven rack for 5 minutes.

CUT soufflé into serving pieces. Serve with fruit.

Vanilla Croquettes in Fruit Sauce

Vanillekroketten mit Fruchtsoßen

Recipe No. 744

Ingredients:

1 pkg	**oetker** vanilla pudding (43 g)	1	pkg
375 mL	milk	1½	cups
50 g	sugar	¼	cup

Coating:

some	flour		some
2	eggs, lightly beaten	2	
120 g	bread crumbs	1	cup

Deep Frying:

some	vegetable oil		some

Raspberry Sauce:

250 g	raspberries	2	cups
70 g	sugar	⅓	cup

Peach Sauce:

1 can	peaches (398 mL/14 fl oz)	1	can
some	rum		some

Decoration:

some	yogurt		some

PREPARE pudding according to package directions using only 375 mL (1½ cups) of milk. POUR into a bowl. Cover with plastic wrap to prevent skin from forming. Chill.

PLACE pudding in a pastry bag fitted with a large plain tube. Squeeze strips of pudding onto a baking sheet. Cool completely.

CUT into 5 cm (2") long pieces.

COAT pieces with flour, then with beaten eggs and finally with bread crumbs.

FILL a deep fryer half way with vegetable oil. HEAT slowly. During the frying process the temperature should be kept at a constant, 180°C (350°F).

PLACE croquettes in hot oil. Deep fry until golden.

REMOVE from oil with a slotted spoon and drain on paper towels.

PLACE croquettes on wire cooling rack.

Raspberry Sauce:
IN a blender, puree raspberries and sugar.

Peach Sauce:
IN a blender, puree peaches and rum. TRANSFER croquettes to dessert plates. SERVE with fruit sauces. SWIRL yogurt through sauce.

Rhubarb Bundles

Rhabarbersäckchen mit Bierzabaione

Recipe No. 745

Ingredients:

1 pkg	frozen phyllo or puff pastry dough	1	pkg

Filling:

2-3 stems	rhubarb	2-3	stems
15 mL	honey	1	tbsp
15 mL	sugar	1	tbsp
1 mL	cinnamon	¼	tsp

Deep Frying:

some	vegetable oil		some

Beer Sauce:

250 mL	dark beer	1	cup
45 mL	honey	3	tbsp
1 pkg	**oetker** vanilla sugar (9 g)	1	pkg
15 mL	icing sugar, sifted	1	tbsp
5	egg yolks	5	
2 mL	lemon juice	½	tsp

THAW pastry according to package directions.
USING a pizza cutter, cut out circles 15 cm (6") in diameter.

Filling:

CUT rhubarb into 2 cm (1") pieces. Place pieces in a heat resistant casserole dish.
ADD honey and sugar. Mix well. Marinate for 30 minutes.
PREHEAT oven to 160°C (325°F).
BAKE for 10-12 minutes.
REMOVE from heat. Cool completely.
ADD cinnamon.
PLACE a small amount of the rhubarb mixture in the centre of each circle.
BRUSH edge of circles lightly with water.
FOLD pastry around the filling to form little bundles. Press together at top.
FILL a deep fryer half way with vegetable oil.
HEAT slowly. During the frying process the temperature should be kept at a constant, 180°C (350°F). Place bundles in hot oil.
DEEP fry until golden.
REMOVE from oil with a slotted spoon and drain on paper towels. Cool on wire rack.

Beer Sauce:

IN a double boiler, beat beer, honey, vanilla sugar, icing sugar, egg yolks and lemon juice until thick and fluffy.
SERVE rhubarb bundles with beer sauce.

117

Frankfurt Pudding

Frankfurter Pudding

Recipe No. 746

Ingredients:

300	g	graham cracker crumbs	2½ cups
60	mL	kirsch (cherry brandy)	4 tbsp
60	mL	rum	4 tbsp
225	g	butter, softened	1 cup
250	g	sugar	1¼ cups
9		egg yolks	9
9		egg whites	9
150	g	almonds, ground	1½ cups

Bishop's Sauce:

250	mL	water	1 cup
250	g	sugar	1¼ cups
		juice of 2 oranges	
2	mL	cinnamon	½ tsp
1	mL	salt	¼ tsp
		peel of 2 oranges	
		peel of 1 lemon	
45	mL	**oetker** Gustin corn starch	3 tbsp
50	mL	rum	¼ cup
100	g	sultana raisins	⅔ cup
55	g	pine nuts	⅓ cup
750	mL	red wine	3 cups

GREASE muffin tins. Sprinkle lightly with sugar.

SOAK graham cracker crumbs in a mixture of kirsch and rum. Cover. Let stand for 30 minutes.

IN a mixing bowl, beat butter and half the sugar until fluffy.

ADD egg yolks, one at a time, beating well after each addition.

IN another bowl, beat egg whites and remaining sugar to stiff peaks.

SPOON beaten egg white mixture, graham cracker mixture and almonds over the butter mixture.

FOLD in gently but thoroughly.

PREHEAT oven to 180°C (350°F).

TURN mixture into prepared tins.

FILL a baking pan halfway with water. Place muffin tins in the pan.

BAKE for 45-50 minutes. Cool.

Bishop's Sauce

IN a saucepan, combine water, sugar, orange juice, cinnamon and salt.

ZEST the orange and lemon into fine strips.

ADD to water mixture. Bring to a boil. Cool completely.

STIR in corn starch.

ADD rum, raisins, pine nuts and wine. Bring to a boil.

TURN pudding onto baking sheet. Transfer to dessert plates. Serve with warm sauce.

Dumplings in Peach Sauce

Grießknödel mit Pfirsichschaum

Recipe No. 747

Ingredients:

750 mL	milk	3	cups
	pinch salt		pinch
	pinch sugar		pinch
250 g	cream of wheat	1¼	cups
3	eggs	3	

Peach Sauce:

3	peaches, peeled	3	
250 mL	white wine	1	cup
3	egg yolks	3	
1 pkg	**oetker** vanilla sugar (9 g)	1	pkg
50 g	sugar	¼	cup

Rolling:

some	sugar	some	
some	cinnamon	some	

IN a saucepan, bring milk, salt and sugar to a boil.

ADD cream of wheat, stirring constantly.

COOK, over low heat, for 10-15 minutes.

COVER and let rest for approximately 20 minutes.

STIR eggs into the cooled mixture, one at a time. Chill.

MOISTEN hands. Shape mixture into small dumplings.

PLACE dumplings in simmering salted water and poach for approximately 10 minutes.

Peach Sauce:

IN a saucepan, cook peaches in 125 mL (½ cup) of the wine until soft.

IN a blender, puree mixture.

IN a double boiler, beat egg yolks, vanilla sugar, sugar and remaining wine until fluffy.

ADD pureed peaches.

HEAT mixture to a temperature of 70°C (150°F), stirring constantly.

SPOON peach sauce onto dessert plates.

ROLL dumplings in a mixture of sugar and cinnamon.

SERVE dumplings on peach sauce.

Cream Cheese Dumplings

Mährische Topfenknödel

Recipe No. 748

Ingredients:

60	g	butter	¹/₄	cup
60	g	sugar	¹/₄	cup
1		egg	1	
	pinch	salt		pinch
250	g	cream cheese	1	cup
80	g	cream of wheat	¹/₃	cup
80	g	all-purpose flour	²/₃	cup

Topping:

60	g	butter	¹/₄	cup
30	mL	honey	2	tbsp
120	g	poppy seed, ground	1¹/₄	cups

IN a mixing bowl, beat butter, sugar, egg, salt and cream cheese until smooth.

BEAT in cream of wheat and flour. Let rest for 1 hour.

MOISTEN hands. Shape mixture into small dumplings.

PLACE dumplings in simmering salted water.

POACH for 10-12 minutes.

IN a saucepan, heat butter and honey.

ADD poppy seeds.

USING a slotted spoon, remove dumplings from water. Drain.

TRANSFER to dessert plates.

SPOON poppy seed mixture over dumplings.

*S*now Dumplings with Summer Berries

*S*chneebällchen mit Beerencocktail

Recipe No. 749

Ingredients:

4		egg whites	4	
1	mL	cream of tartar	¹/₄	tsp
120	g	sugar	¹/₂	cup
1	pkg	**oetker** vanilla sugar (9 g)	1	pkg
500	mL	milk	2	cups

Vanilla Sauce:

1	pkg	**oetker** instant vanilla sauce (35 g)	1	pkg
250	mL	milk	1	cup

Berry Cocktail:

500	g	mixed berries	4	cups
	some	sugar		some

IN a mixing bowl, beat egg whites and cream of tartar until soft peaks form.
GRADUALLY beat in sugar and vanilla sugar until stiff peaks form.
IN a saucepan, bring milk to a simmer.
USING a tablespoon, scoop meringue into small balls.
DROP two to three balls into the saucepan.
POACH for 2 minutes. Turn meringues over and poach 2-3 minutes longer.
USING a slotted spoon, remove snow dumplings. Drain.

Vanilla Sauce:
PREPARE vanilla sauce according to package directions.
POUR sauce onto dessert plates.
PLACE two or three snow dumplings in the sauce.

Berry Cocktail:
SWEETEN berries with sugar.
SERVE with snow dumplings.

Quark and Apple Soufflé

Topfenauflauf mit Äpfeln

Recipe No. 750

Ingredients:

4	apples	4	
400 g	quark	1½	cups
3	egg yolks	3	
50 mL	butter, melted	¼	cup
30 mL	rum	2	tbsp
50 g	raisins	⅓	cup
	juice and peel of 1 lemon		
3	egg whites	3	
110 g	sugar	½	cup
1 pkg	**oetker** vanilla pudding (9 g)	1	pkg
2 mL	**oetker** baking powder	½	tsp

Sprinkling:

15 mL	sugar	1	tbsp
2 mL	cinnamon	½	tsp

PREHEAT oven to 180°C (350°F). Grease a 28 x 43 cm (11 x 17") casserole dish.
WASH, peel, core and cube apples.
SPREAD apples evenly in the bottom of the prepared casserole dish.
IN a mixing bowl, beat quark, egg yolks, butter, rum, raisins, lemon juice and peel.
IN another bowl, beat egg whites and sugar to stiff peaks.
MIX together pudding and baking powder.
SIFT over beaten egg white.
FOLD into quark mixture gently but thoroughly.
SPREAD quark mixture evenly over the apples in the casserole dish.
MIX together sugar and cinnamon.
SPRINKLE over surface of quark mixture.
BAKE for 45-50 minutes.
COOL slightly. Serve warm.

*R*ecipe Index

The **oetker** *Library of Baking*

Baking is Fun — The ABC's of Baking This book will guide you through a variety of baking techniques. Learn how to prepare batters, doughs, fillings and glazes. Complete with decorating ideas and helpful hints.

Baking Is Fun — Volume 1 (Recipes No. 1 - 93) Prepare Traditional European desserts such as Black Forest Cake, Hazelnut Cream Torte and Apple Strudel with the aid of this book.

Baking Is Fun — Volume 2 (Recipes No. 94 - 190) A unique collection of European baking specialties.

Baking Is Fun — Volume 3 (Recipes No. 191 - 270) This volume consists of Traditional Holiday recipes for the Christmas season. This volume also contains a special section on recipes for diabetics.

Baking Is Fun — Volume 4 (Recipes No. 271 - 350) Light Wholesome Baking is the principal theme of Volume 4. Make a soufflé, a specialty bread or a gourmet dessert. There are many recipes to choose from.

Baking Is Fun — Volume 5 (Recipes No. 351 - 433) This volume contains a rich assortment of tempting yeast recipes.

Baking Is Fun — Volume 6 (Recipes No. 434 - 513) This volume, entitled "Specialties of the World", takes you on a culinary trip around the world with recipes from Austria to Australia and China to Sicily.

Baking Is Fun — Volume 7 (Recipes No. 514 - 593) This volume contains many Classic European recipes.

Baking Is Fun — Volume 8 (Recipes No. 594 - 678) A collection of tantalizing cookie recipes . . . from sweet to savoury. Something for every taste and temptation.

Baking Is Fun — Volume 9 (Recipes No. 679 - 750) Tempt your palate with a unique variety of enticing dessert recipes prepared with fruit.

To order these books please write to:

oetker Recipe Service
2229 Drew Road
Mississauga, Ontario
L5S 1E5

Personal Notes

*P*ersonal Notes

128